# Kitchen Elegance:

# Inspired Dishes Collection

# By

# Dorothy A. Williams

## SOUP, Brilla.

*Ingredients.*—4 lbs. of shin of beef, 3 carrots, 2 turnips, a large sprig of thyme, 2 onions, 1 head of celery, salt and pepper to taste, 4 quarts water. *Mode.*—Take the beef, cut off all the meat from the bone, in nice square pieces, and boil the bone for 4 hours. Strain the liquor, let it cool, and take off the fat; then put the pieces of meat in the cold liquor; cut small the carrots, turnips, and celery; chop the onions, add them with the thyme and seasoning, and simmer till the meat is tender. If not brown enough, colour it with browning. *Time.*—6 hours. *Average cost*, 5*d.* per quart. *Seasonable* all the year. *Sufficient* for 10 persons.

## SOUP, Chantilly.

*Ingredients.*—1 quart of young green peas, a small bunch of parsley, 2 young onions, 2 quarts of medium stock. *Mode.*—Boil the peas till quite tender, with the parsley and onions; then rub them through a sieve, and pour the stock to them. Do not let it boil after the peas are added, or you will spoil the colour. Serve very hot. *Time.*—½ hour. *Average cost*, 1*s.* 6*d.* per quart. *Seasonable* from June to the end of August. *Sufficient* for 8 persons.

*Note.*—Cold peas pounded in a mortar, with a little stock added to them, make a very good soup in haste.

## SOUP, Calf's-head.

*Ingredients.*—½ of calf's head, 1 onion stuck with cloves, a very small bunch of sweet herbs, 2 blades of mace, salt and white pepper to taste, 6 oz. of rice-flour, 3 tablespoonfuls of ketchup, 3 quarts of white stock, or pot-liquor, or water. *Mode.*—Rub the head with salt, soak it for 6 hours, and clean it thoroughly, put it in the stewpan, and cover it with the stock, or pot-liquor, or water, adding the onion and sweet herbs. When well skimmed and boiled for 1½ hour, take out the head, and skim and strain the soup. Mix the rice-flour with the ketchup, thicken the soup with it, and simmer for 5 minutes. Now cut up the head into pieces about two inches long, and simmer them in the soup till the meat and fat are quite tender. Season with white pepper and mace finely pounded, and serve very hot. When the calf's head is taken out of the soup, cover it up or it will discolour. *Time.*—2½ hours. *Average cost*, 1*s*. 9*d*. per quart, with stock. *Seasonable* from May to October. *Sufficient* for 10 persons.

*Note.*—Forcemeat balls can be added, and the soup may be flavoured with a little lemon-juice, or a glass of sherry or Madeira. The bones from the head may be stewed down again, with a few fresh vegetables, and it will make a very good common stock.

## SOUP, à la Cantatrice. (An Excellent Soup, very Beneficial for the Voice.)

*Ingredient.*—3 oz. of sago, ½ pint of cream, the yolks of 3 eggs, 1 lump of sugar, and seasoning to taste, 1 bay-leaf (if liked), 2 quarts of medium stock. *Mode.*—Having washed the sago in boiling water, let it be gradually added to the nearly boiling stock. Simmer for ½ hour, when it should be well dissolved. Beat up the yolks of the eggs, add to them the boiling cream; stir these quickly in the soup, and serve immediately. Do not let the soup boil, or the eggs will curdle. *Time.*—40 minutes. *Average cost*, 1*s*. 6*d*. per quart. *Seasonable* all the year. *Sufficient* for 8 persons.

*Note.*—This is a soup, the principal ingredients of which, sago and eggs, have always been deemed very beneficial to the chest and throat. In various quantities, and in different preparations, these have been partaken of by the principal singers of the day, including the celebrated Swedish Nightingale, Jenny Lind, and, as they have always avowed, with considerable advantage to the voice, in singing.

## SOUP, à la Crécy.

*Ingredients.*—4 carrots, 2 sliced onions, 1 cut lettuce, and chervil; 2 oz. butter, 1 pint of lentils, the crumbs of 2 French rolls, half a teacupful of rice, 2 quarts of medium stock. *Mode.*—Put the vegetables with the butter in the stewpan, and let them simmer 5 minutes; then add the lentils and 1 pint of the stock, and stew gently for half an hour. Now fill it up with the remainder of the stock, let it boil another hour, and put in the crumb of the rolls. When well soaked, rub all through a tammy. Have ready the rice boiled; pour the soup over this, and serve. *Time.*—1¾ hour. *Average cost,* 1*s.* 2*d.* per quart. *Seasonable* all the year. *Sufficient* for 8 persons.

## SOUP, à la Flamande (Flemish).

*Ingredients.*—1 turnip, 1 small carrot, ½ head of celery, 6 green onions shred very fine, 1 lettuce cut small, chervil, ¼ pint of asparagus cut small, ¼ pint of peas, 2 oz. butter, the yolks of 4 eggs, ½ pint of cream, salt to taste, 1 lump of sugar, 2 quarts of stock. *Mode.*—Put the vegetables in the butter to stew gently for an hour with a teacupful of stock; then add the remainder of the stock, and simmer for another hour. Now beat the yolks of the eggs well, mix with the cream (previously boiled), and strain through a hair sieve. Take the soup off the fire, put the eggs, &c., to it and keep stirring it well. Bring it almost to boiling point, but do not leave off stirring, or the eggs will curdle. Season with salt, and add the sugar. *Time.*—2½ hours. *Average cost,* 1*s.* 9*d.* per quart. *Seasonable* from May to August. *Sufficient* for 8 persons.

## SOUP, à la Flamande (Flemish).

*Ingredients.*—5 onions, 5 heads of celery, 10 moderate-sized potatoes, 3 oz. butter, ½ pint of water, ½ pint of cream, 2 quarts of stock. *Mode.*—Slice the onions, celery, and potatoes, and put them with the butter and water into a stewpan, and simmer for an hour. Then fill up the stewpan with stock, and boil gently till the potatoes are done, which will be in about an hour. Rub all through a tammy, and add the cream (previously boiled). Do not let it boil after the cream is put in. *Time.*—2½ hours. *Average cost,* 1*s.* 4*d.* per quart. *Seasonable* from September to May. *Sufficient* for 8 persons.

*Note.*—This soup can be made with water instead of stock.

## SOUP, a Good Family .

*Ingredients.*—Remains of a cold tongue, 2 lbs. of shin of beef, any cold pieces of meat or beef-bones, 2 turnips, 2 carrots, 2 onions, 1 parsnip, 1 head of celery, 4 quarts of water, ½ teacupful of rice; salt and pepper to taste. *Mode.*—Put all the ingredients in a stewpan, and simmer gently for 4 hours, or until all the goodness is drawn from the meat. Strain off the soup, and let it stand to get cold. The kernels and soft parts of the tongue must be saved. When the soup is wanted for use, skim off all the fat, put in the kernels and soft parts of the tongue, slice in a small quantity of fresh carrot, turnip, and onion; stew till the vegetables are tender, and serve with toasted bread. *Time.*—5 hours. *Averagecost*, 3d. per quart. *Seasonable* at any time. *Sufficient* for 12 persons.

## SOUP, Hessian.

*Ingredients.*—Half an ox's head, 1 pint of split peas, 8 carrots, 6 turnips, 6 potatoes, 6 onions, 1 head of celery, 1 bunch of savoury herbs, pepper and salt to taste, 2 blades of mace, a little allspice, 4 cloves, the crumb of a French roll, 6 quarts of water. *Mode.*—Clean the head, rub it with salt and water, and soak it for 5 hours in warm water. Simmer it in the water till tender, put it into a pan and let it cool; skim off all the fat; take out the head, and add the vegetables cut up small, and the peas which have been previously soaked; simmer them without the meat, till they are done enough to pulp through a sieve. Put in the seasoning, with the pieces of meat cut up; give one boil, and serve. *Time.*—4 hours. *Average cost*, 6d. per quart. *Seasonable* in winter. *Sufficient* for 16 persons.

*Note.*—An excellent hash or *ragoût* can be made by cutting up the nicest parts of the head, thickening and seasoning more highly a little of the soup, and adding a glass of port wine and 2 tablespoonfuls of ketchup.

## SOUP, Portable.

*Ingredients.*—2 knuckles of veal, 3 shins of beef, 1 large faggot of herbs, 2 bay-leaves, 2 heads of celery, 3 onions, 3 carrots, 2 blades of mace, 6 cloves, a teaspoonful of salt, sufficient water to cover all the ingredients. *Mode.*—Take the marrow from the bones; put all the ingredients in a stock-pot, and simmer slowly for 12 hours, or more, if the meat be not done to rags; strain it off, and put it in a very cool place; take off all the fat, reduce the liquor in a shallow pan, by setting it over a sharp fire, but be particular that it does not burn; boil it fast and uncovered for 8 hours, and keep it stirred. Put it into a deep dish, and set it by for a day. Have ready a stewpan of boiling water, place the dish in it, and keep it boiling; stir occasionally, and when the soup is thick and ropy, it is done. Form it into little cakes by pouring a small quantity on to the bottom of cups or basins; when cold, turn them out on a flannel to dry. Keep them from the air in tin canisters. *Averagecost* of this quantity, 16s.

*Note.*—Soup can be made in 5 minutes with this, by dissolving a small piece, about the size of a walnut, in a pint of warm water, and simmering for 2 minutes. Vermicelli, macaroni, or other Italian pastes, may be added.

## SOUP, Prince of Wales's.

*Ingredients.*—12 turnips, 1 lump of sugar, 2 spoonfuls of strong veal stock, salt and white pepper to taste, 2 quarts of very bright stock. *Mode.*—Peel the turnips, and with a cutter cut them in balls as round as possible, but very small. Put them in the stock, which must be very bright, and simmer till tender. Add the veal stock and seasoning. Have little pieces of bread cut round, about the size of a shilling; moisten them with stock; put them into a tureen and pour the soup over without shaking, for fear of crumbling the bread, which would spoil the appearance of the soup, and make it look thick. *Time.*—2 hours. *Seasonable* in the winter. *Sufficient* for 8 persons.

## SOUP, Regency.

*Ingredients.*—The bones and remains of any cold game such as of pheasants, partridges, &c.; 2 carrots, 2 small onions, 1 head of celery, 1 turnip, ¼ lb. of pearl barley, the yolks of 3 eggs boiled hard, ¼ pint of cream, salt to taste, 2 quarts of medium or common stock. *Mode.*—Place the bones or remains of game in the stewpan, with the vegetables sliced; pour over the stock, and simmer for 2 hours; skim off all the fat, and strain it. Wash the barley, and boil it in 2 or 3 waters before putting it to the soup; finish simmering in the soup, and when the barley is done, take out half, and pound the other half with the yolks of the eggs. When you have finished pounding, rub it through a clean tammy, add the cream, and salt if necessary; give one boil, and serve very hot, putting in the barley that was taken out first. *Time.*—2½ hours. *Average cost*, 1s. per quart, if made with medium stock, or 6d. per quart, with common stock. *Seasonable* from September to March. *Sufficient* for 8 persons.

### SOUP, à la Reine.

*Ingredients.*—1 large fowl, 1 oz. of sweet almonds, the crumb of 1½ French roll, ½ pint of cream, salt to taste, 1 small lump of sugar, 2 quarts of good white veal stock. *Mode.*—Boil the fowl gently in the stock till quite tender, which will be in about an hour, or rather more; take out the fowl, pull the meat from the bones, and put it into a mortar with the almonds, and pound very fine. When beaten enough, put the meat back in the stock, with the crumb of the rolls, and let it simmer for an hour; rub it through a tammy, add the sugar, ½ pint of cream that has boiled, and, if you prefer, cut the crust of the roll into small round pieces, and pour the soup over it, when you serve. *Time.*—2 hours, or rather more. *Average cost*, 2s. 7d. per quart. *Seasonable* all the year. *Sufficient* for 8 persons.

*Note.*—All white soups should be warmed in a vessel placed in another of boiling water.

### SOUP, à la Reine (Economical).

*Ingredients.*—Any remains of roast chickens, ½ teacupful of rice, salt and pepper to taste, 1 quart of stock. *Mode.*—Take all the white meat and pound it with the rice, which has been slightly cooked, but not too much. When it is all well pounded, dilute with the stock, and pass through a sieve. This soup should neither be too clear nor too thick. *Time.*—1 hour. *Average cost*, 4d. per quart. *Seasonable* all the year. *Sufficient* for 4 persons.

*Note.*—If stock is not at hand, put the chicken-bones in water, with an onion, carrot, a few sweet herbs, a blade of mace, pepper and salt, and stew for 3 hours.

### SOUP, à la Solferino (Sardinian Recipe).

*Ingredients.*—4 eggs, ½ pint of cream, 2 oz. of fresh butter, salt and pepper to taste, a little flour to thicken, 2 quarts of bouillon. *Mode.*—Beat the eggs, put them into a stewpan, and add the cream, butter, and seasoning; stir in as much flour as will bring it to the consistency of dough; make it into balls, either round or egg-shaped, and fry them in butter; put them in the tureen, and pour the boiling bouillon over them. *Time.*—1 hour. *Average cost*, 1*s.* 3*d.* per quart. *Seasonable* all the year. *Sufficient* for 8 persons.

*Note.*—This recipe was communicated to the Editress by an English gentleman, who was present at the battle of Solferino, on June 24, 1859, and who was requested by some of Victor Emmanuel's troops, on the day before the battle, to partake of a portion of their *potage*. He willingly enough consented, and found that these clever campaigners had made a palatable dish from very easily-procured materials. In sending the recipe for insertion in this work, he has, however, Anglicised, and somewhat, he thinks, improved it.

## SOUP, Spring, or Potage Printanier.

*Ingredients.*—½ a pint of green peas, if in season, a little chervil, 2 shredded lettuces, 2 onions, a very small bunch of parsley, 2 oz. of butter, the yolks of 3 eggs, 1 pint of water, seasoning to taste, 2 quarts of stock. *Mode.*—Put in a clean stewpan the chervil, lettuces, onions, parsley, and butter, to 1 pint of water, and let them simmer till tender. Season with salt and pepper; when done, strain off the vegetables, and put two-thirds of the liquor they were boiled in to the stock. Beat up the yolks of the eggs with the other third, give it a toss over the fire, and at the moment of serving, add this, with the vegetables which you strained off, to the soup. *Time.*—¾ of an hour. *Average cost*, 1*s.* per quart. *Seasonable* from May to October. *Sufficient* for 8 persons.

## SOUP, Stew.

*Ingredients.*—2 lbs. of beef, 5 onions, 5 turnips, ¾ lb. of rice, a large bunch of parsley, a few sweet herbs, pepper and salt, 2 quarts of water. *Mode.*—Cut the beef up in small pieces, add the other ingredients, and boil gently for 2½ hours. Oatmeal or potatoes would be a great improvement. *Time.*—2½ hours. *Average cost*, 6*d.* per quart. *Seasonable* in winter. *Sufficient* for 6 persons.

## SOUP, Stew.

*Ingredients.*—½ lb. of beef, mutton, or pork; ½ pint of split peas, 4 turnips, 8 potatoes, 2 onions, 2 oz. of oatmeal or 3 oz. of rice, 2 quarts of water. *Mode.*—Cut the meat in small pieces, as also the vegetables, and add them, with the peas, to the water. Boil gently for 3 hours; thicken with the oatmeal, boil for another ¼ hour, stirring all the time, and season with pepper and salt. *Time.*—3¼ hours. *Average cost*, 4*d.* per quart. *Seasonable* in winter. *Sufficient* for 8 persons.

*Note.*—This soup may be made of the liquor in which tripe has been boiled, by adding vegetables, seasoning, rice, &c.

## SOUP, Stew, of Salt Meat.

*Ingredients.*—Any pieces of salt beef or pork, say 2 lbs.; 4 carrots, 4 parsnips, 4 turnips, 4 potatoes, 1 cabbage, 2 oz. of oatmeal or ground rice, seasoning of salt and pepper, 2 quarts of water. *Mode.*—Cut up the meat small, add the water, and let it simmer for 2¾ hours. Now add the vegetables, cut in thin small slices; season, and boil for 1 hour. Thicken with the oatmeal, and serve. *Time.*—2 hours. *Average cost*, 3*d.* per quart without the meat. *Seasonable* in winter. *Sufficient* for 6 persons.

*Note.*—If rice is used instead of oatmeal, put it in with the vegetables.

## SOUP, Useful for Benevolent Purposes.

*Ingredients.*—An ox-cheek, any pieces of trimmings of beef, which may be bought very cheaply (say 4 lbs.), a few bones, any pot-liquor the larder may furnish, ¼ peck of onions, 6 leeks, a large bunch of herbs, ½ lb. of celery (the outside pieces, or green tops, do very well); ½ lb. of carrots, ½ lb. of turnips, ½ lb. of coarse brown sugar, ½ a pint of beer, 4 lbs. of common rice, or pearl barley; ½ lb. of salt, 1 oz. of black pepper, a few raspings, 10 gallons of water. *Mode.*—Divide the meat in small pieces, break the bones, put them in a copper, with the 10 gallons of water, and stew for half an hour. Cut up the vegetables, put them in with the sugar and beer, and boil for 4 hours. Two hours before the soup is wanted, add the rice and raspings, and keep stirring till they are well mixed in the soup, which simmer gently. If the liquor boils away a little, fill up with water. *Time.*—6½ hours. *Average cost*, 1½*d.* per quart.

## SOUP, White.

*Ingredients.*—¼ lb. of sweet almonds, ¼ lb. of cold veal or poultry, a thick slice of stale bread, a piece of fresh lemon-peel, 1 blade of mace, pounded, ¾ pint of cream, the yolks of 2 hard-boiled eggs, 2 quarts of white stock. *Mode.*—Reduce the almonds in a mortar to a paste, with a spoonful of water, and add to them the meat, which should be previously pounded with the bread. Beat all together, and add the lemon-peel, very finely chopped, and the mace. Pour the boiling stock on the whole, and simmer for an hour. Rub the eggs in the cream, put in the soup, bring it to a boil, and serve immediately. *Time.*—1½ hour. *Average cost*, 1*s.* 6*d.* per quart. *Seasonable* all the year. *Sufficient* for 8 persons.

*Note.*—-A more economical white soup may be made by using common veal stock, and thickening with rice, flour, and milk. Vermicelli should be served with it. *Averagecost* , 5*d.* per quart.

## SPINACH, to Boil (English Mode).

*Ingredients.*—2 pailfuls of spinach, 2 heaped tablespoonfuls of salt, 1 oz. of of butter, pepper to taste. *Mode.*—Pick the spinach carefully, and see that no stalks or weeds are left amongst it; wash it in several waters, and, to prevent it being gritty, act in the following manner:—Have ready two large pans or tubs filled with water; put the spinach into one of these, and thoroughly wash it; then, *with the hands*, take out the spinach, and put it into the *other tub* of water (by this means all the grit will be left at the-bottom of the tub); wash it again, and should it not be perfectly free from dirt, repeat the process. Put it into a very large saucepan, with about ½ pint of water, just sufficient to keep the spinach from burning, and the above proportion of salt. Press it down frequently with a wooden spoon, that it may be done equally; and when it has boiled for rather more than 10 minutes, or until it is perfectly tender, drain it in a colander, squeeze it quite dry, and chop it finely. Put the spinach into a clean stewpan, with the butter and a seasoning of pepper; stir the whole over the fire until quite hot; then put it on a hot dish, and garnish with sippets of toasted bread. *Time.*—10 to 15 minutes to boil the spinach, 5 minutes to warm with the butter. *Average cost* for the above quantity, 8*d.* *Sufficient* for 5 or 6 persons. *Seasonable.*—

Spring spinach from March to July; winter spinach from November to March.

SPINACH GARNISHED WITH CROÛTONS.

*Note.*—Grated nutmeg, pounded mace, or lemon-juice may also be added to enrich the flavour; and poached eggs are also frequently served with spinach: they should be placed on the top of it, and it should be garnished with sippets of toasted bread.

## SPINACH dressed with Cream, à la Française.

*Ingredients.*—2 pailfuls of spinach, 2 tablespoonfuls of salt, 2 oz. of butter, 8 tablespoonfuls of cream, 1 small teaspoonful of pounded sugar, a very little grated nutmeg. *Mode.*—Boil and drain the spinach; chop it fine, and put it into a stewpan with the butter; stir it over a gentle fire, and, when the butter has dried away, add the remaining ingredients, and simmer for about 5 minutes. Previously to pouring in the cream, boil it first, in case it should curdle. Serve on a hot dish, and garnish either with sippets of toasted bread or leaves of puff-paste. *Time.*—10 to 15 minutes to boil the spinach; 10 minutes to stew with the cream. *Average cost* for the above quantity, 8*d*. *Sufficient* for 5 or 6 persons. *Seasonable.*—Spring spinach from March to July; winter spinach from November to March.

## SPINACH, French Mode of Dressing.

*Ingredients.*—2 pailfuls of spinach, 2 tablespoonfuls of salt, 2 oz. of butter, 1 teaspoonful of flour, 8 tablespoonfuls of good gravy; when liked, a very little grated nutmeg. *Mode.*—Pick, wash, and boil the spinach, and when tender, drain and squeeze it perfectly dry from the water that hangs about it. Chop it very fine, put the butter into a stewpan, and lay the spinach over that; stir it over a gentle fire, and dredge in the flour. Add the gravy, and let it boil *quickly* for a few minutes, that it may not discolour. When the flavour of nutmeg is liked, grate some to the spinach, and when thoroughly hot, and the gravy has dried away a little, serve. Garnish the dish with sippets of toasted bread. *Time.*—10 to 15 minutes to boil the spinach; 10

minutes to simmer in the gravy. *Average cost* for the above quantity, 8*d*. *Sufficient* for 5 or 6 persons. *Seasonable.*—Spring spinach from March to July; winter spinach from October to February.

*Note.*—For an *entremets* or second-course dish, spinach dressed by the above recipe may be pressed into a hot mould; it should then be turned out quickly, and served immediately.

## SPINACH-GREEN, for Colouring various Dishes.

*Ingredients.*—2 handfuls of spinach. *Mode.*—Pick and wash the spinach free from dirt, and pound the leaves in a mortar to extract the juice; then press it through a hair sieve, and put the juice into a small stewpan or jar. Place this in a bain marie, or saucepan of boiling water, and let it set. Watch it closely, as it should not boil; and, as soon as it is done, lay it in a sieve, so that all the water may drain from it, and the green will then be ready for colouring. If made according to this recipe, the spinach-green will be found far superior to that boiled in the ordinary way.

## SPINACH SOUP (French Recipe).

*Ingredients.*—As much spinach as, when boiled, will half fill a vegetable-dish, 2 quarts of very clear medium stock. *Mode.*—Make the cooked spinach into balls the size of an egg, and slip them into the soup-tureen. This is a very elegant soup, the green of the spinach forming a pretty contrast to the brown gravy. *Time.*—1 hour. *Average cost*, 1*s.* per quart. *Seasonable* from October to June.

## SPONGE-CAKE.

*Ingredients.*—The weight of 8 eggs in pounded loaf sugar, the weight of 5 in flour, the rind of 1 lemon, 1 tablespoonful of brandy. *Mode.*—Put the eggs into one side of the scale, and take the weight of 8 in pounded loaf sugar, and the weight of 5 in good *dry* flour. Separate the yolks from the whites of the eggs; beat the former, put them into a saucepan with the sugar, and let them remain over the fire until *milk-warm*, keeping them well stirred. Then put them into a basin, add the grated lemon-rind mixed with the brandy, and stir these well together, dredging in the flour very gradually.

Whisk the whites of the eggs to a very stiff froth, stir them to the flour, &c., and beat the cake well for ¼ hour. Put it into a buttered mould strewn with a little fine-sifted sugar, and bake the cake in a quick oven for 1½ hour. Care must be taken that it is put into the oven immediately, or it will not be light. The flavouring of this cake may he varied by adding a few drops of essence of almonds instead of the grated lemon-rind. *Time.*—1½ hour. *Averagecost ,* 1*s.* 3*d. Sufficient* for 1 cake. *Seasonable* at any time.

**SPONGE-CAKE.**

## SPONGE-CAKE.

*Ingredients.*—½ lb. of loaf sugar, not quite ¼ pint of water, 5 eggs, 1 lemon, ½ lb. of flour, ¼ teaspoonful of carbonate of soda. *Mode.*—Boil the sugar and water together until they form a thick syrup; let it cool a little, then pour it to the eggs, which should be previously well whisked; and after the eggs and syrup are mixed together, continue beating them for a few minutes. Grate the lemon-rind, mix the carbonate of soda with the flour, and stir these lightly to the other ingredients; then add the lemon-juice, and, when the whole is thoroughly mixed, pour it into a buttered mould, and bake in rather a quick oven for rather more than 1 hour. The remains of sponge or Savoy cakes answer very well for trifles, light puddings, &c.; and a very stale one (if not mouldy) makes an excellent tipsy cake. *Time.*—Rather more than 1 hour. *Average cost,* 10*d. Sufficient* to make 1 cake. *Seasonable* at any time.

## SPONGE-CAKES,Small.

*Ingredients.*—The weight of 5 eggs in flour, the weight of 8 in pounded loaf sugar; flavouring to taste. *Mode.*—Let the flour be perfectly dry, and the sugar well pounded and sifted. Separate the whites from the yolks of the eggs, and beat the latter up with the sugar; then whisk the whites until they become rather stiff, and mix them with the yolks, but do not stir them more than is just necessary to mingle the ingredients well together. Dredge in the flour by degrees, add the flavouring; butter the tins well, pour in the batter, sift a little sugar over the cakes, and bake them in rather a quick oven, but do not allow them to take too much colour, as they should be rather pale. Remove them from the tins before they get cold, and turn them on their faces, where let them remain until quite cold, when store them away in a closed tin canister or wide-mouthed glass bottle. *Time.*—10 to 15 minutes in a quick oven. *Averagecost*, 1*d.* each. *Seasonable* at any time.

## SPRATS.

Sprats should be cooked very fresh, which can be ascertained by their bright and sparkling eyes. Wipe them dry; fasten them in rows by a skewer run through the eyes; dredge with flour, and broil them on a gridiron over a nice clear fire. The gridiron should be rubbed with suet. Serve very hot. *Time.*—3 or 4 minutes. *Average cost*, 1*d.* per lb. *Seasonable* from November to March.

To Choose Sprats.—Choose these from their silvery appearance, as the brighter they are, so are they the fresher.

## SPRATS,Dried.

Dried sprats should be put into a basin, and boiling water poured over them; they may then be skinned and served, and this will be found a much better way than boiling them.

## SPRATS,FriedinBatter .

*Ingredients.*—2 eggs, flour, bread-crumbs; seasoning of salt and pepper to taste. *Mode.*—Wipe the sprats, and dip them in a batter made of the above ingredients. Fry of a nice brown, serve very hot, and garnish with fried parsley. Sprats may be baked like herrings.

## SPROUTS,toBoilY oung.

*Ingredients.*—To each ½ gallon of water allow 1 heaped tablespoonful of salt; a *verysmall* piece of soda. *Mode.*—Pick away all the dead leaves, and wash the greens well in cold water; drain them in a colander, and put them into fast-boiling water, with salt and soda in the above proportion. Keep them boiling quickly, with the lid uncovered, until tender; and the moment they are done, take them up, or their colour will be spoiled; when well drained, serve. The great art in cooking greens properly, and to have them a good colour, is to put them into *plenty of fast-boiling* water, to let them boil very quickly, and to take them up the moment they become tender. *Time.*—Brocoli sprouts, 10 to 12 minutes; young greens, 10 to 12 minutes; sprouts, 12 minutes, after the water boils. *Seasonable.*—Sprouts of various kinds may be had all the year.

## STEW, Irish.

*Ingredients.*—3 lbs. of the loin or neck of mutton, 5 lbs. of potatoes, 5 large onions, pepper and salt to taste, rather more than 1 pint of water. *Mode.*—Trim off some of the fat of the above quantity of loin or neck of mutton, and cut it into chops of a moderate thickness. Pare and halve the potatoes, and cut the onions into thick slices. Put a layer of potatoes at the bottom of a stewpan, then a layer of mutton and onions, and season with pepper and salt; proceed in this manner until the stewpan is full, taking care to have plenty of vegetables at the top. Pour in the water, and let it stew very gently for 2½ hours, keeping the lid of the stewpan closely shut the *whole* time, and occasionally shaking the preparation to prevent its burning. *Time.*—2½ hours. *Average cost,* for this quantity, 2s. 8d. *Sufficient* for 5 or 6 persons. *Seasonable.*—Suitable for a winter dish.

## STEW, Irish.

*Ingredients.*—2 or 3 lbs. of the breast of mutton, 1½ pint of water, salt and pepper to taste, 4 lbs. of potatoes, 4 large onions. *Mode.*—Put the mutton into a stewpan with the water and a little salt, and let it stew gently for an hour; cut the meat into small pieces, skim the fat from the gravy, and pare and slice the potatoes and onions. Put all the ingredients into the stewpan, in layers, first a layer of vegetables, then one of meat, and sprinkle seasoning of pepper and salt between each layer; cover closely, and let the whole stew very gently for 1 hour, or rather more, shaking it frequently to prevent its burning. *Time.*—Rather more than 2 hours. *Averagecost*, 1*s*. 6*d*. *Sufficient* for 5 or 6 persons. *Seasonable.*—Suitable for a winter dish.

*Note.*—Irish stew may be prepared in the same manner as above, but baked in a jar instead of boiled. About 2 hours or rather more in a moderate oven will be sufficient time to bake it.

## STILTONCHEESE.

**STILTON CHEESE.**

Stilton cheese, or British Parmesan, as it is sometimes called, is generally preferred to all other cheeses by those whose authority few will dispute. Those made in May or June are usually served at Christmas; or, to be in prime order, should be kept from 10 to 12 months, or even longer. An artificial ripeness in Stilton cheese is sometimes produced by inserting a small piece of decayed Cheshire into an aperture at the top. From 3 weeks to a month is sufficient time to ripen the cheese. An additional flavour may also be obtained by scooping out a piece from the top, and pouring therein port, sherry, Madeira, or old ale, and letting the cheese absorb these for two or three weeks. But that cheese is the finest which is ripened without any artificial aid, is the opinion of those who are judges in these matters. In serving a Stilton cheese, the top of it should be cut off to form a lid, and a napkin or piece of white paper, with a frill at the top, pinned round. When the cheese goes from table, the lid should be replaced.

## STOCKS for all kinds of Soups (Rich Strong Stock).

*Ingredients.*—4 lbs. of shin of beef, 4 lbs. of knuckle of veal, ¼ lb. of good lean ham; any poultry trimmings; 2 oz. of butter; 3 onions, 3 carrots, 2 turnips (the latter should be omitted in summer, lest they ferment), 1 head of celery, a few chopped mushrooms, when obtainable; 1 tomato, a bunch of savoury herbs, not forgetting parsley; 1½ oz. of salt, 3 lumps of sugar, 12 white peppercorns, 6 cloves, 3 small blades of mace, 4 quarts of water. *Mode.*—Line a delicately clean stewpan with the ham cut in thin broad slices, carefully trimming off all its rusty fat; cut up the beef and veal in pieces about 3 inches square, and lay them on the ham; set it on the stove, and draw it down, and stir frequently. When the meat is equally browned, put in the beef and veal bones, the poultry trimmings, and pour in the cold water. Skim well, and occasionally add a little cold water, to stop its boiling, until it becomes quite clear; then put in all the other ingredients, and simmer very slowly for 5 hours. Do not let it come to a brisk boil, that the stock be not wasted, and that its colour may be preserved. Strain through a very fine hair sieve, or cloth, and the stock will be fit for use. *Time.*—5 hours. *Average cost*, 1*s*. 3*d*. per quart.

## STOCK, Economical.

*Ingredients.*—The liquor in which a joint of meat has been boiled, say 4 quarts; trimmings of fresh meat or poultry, shank-bones, &c., roast-beef bones, any pieces the larder may furnish; vegetables, spices, and the same seasoning as in the foregoing recipe. *Mode.*—Let all the ingredients simmer gently for 6 hours, taking care to skim carefully at first. Strain it off, and put by for use. *Time.*—6 hours. *Average cost*, 3*d*. per quart.

## STOCK, Medium.

*Ingredients.*—4 lbs. of shin of beef, or 4 lbs. of knuckle of veal, or 2 lbs. of each; any bones, trimmings of poultry, or fresh meat, ¼ lb. of lean bacon or ham, 2 oz. of butter, 2 large onions, each stuck with 3 cloves; 1 turnip, 3 carrots, 1 head of celery, 3 lumps of sugar, 2 oz. of salt, ½ a teaspoonful of whole pepper, 1 large blade of mace, 1 bunch of savoury herbs, 4 quarts and ½ pint of cold water. *Mode.*—Cut up the meat and bacon or ham into pieces of about 3 inches square; rub the butter on the bottom of the stewpan; put in ½ a pint of water, the meat, and all the other ingredients. Cover the stewpan, and place it on a sharp fire, occasionally stirring its contents. When the bottom of the pan becomes covered with a pale, jelly-like substance, add the 4 quarts of cold water, and simmer very gently for 5 hours. As we have said before, do not let it boil quickly. Remove every particle of scum whilst it is doing, and strain it through a fine hair sieve. This stock is the basis of most of the soups mentioned in this dictionary, and will be found quite strong enough for ordinary purposes. *Time.*—5½ hours. *Average cost*, 9*d*. per quart.

## STOCK, To Clarify.

*Ingredients.*—The whites of 2 eggs, ½ pint of water, 2 quarts of stock. *Mode.*—Supposing that by some accident the soup is not quite clear, and that its quantity is 2 quarts, take the whites of 2 eggs, carefully separated from their yolks, whisk them well together with the water, and add gradually the 2 quarts of boiling stock, still whisking. Place the soup on the fire, and when boiling and well skimmed, whisk the eggs with it till nearly boiling again; then draw it from the fire, and let it settle, until the whites of the eggs become separated. Pass through a fine cloth, and the soup should be clear.

*Note.*—The rule is, that all clear soups should be of a light straw-colour, and should not savour too strongly of the meat; and that all white or brown thick soups should have no more consistency than will enable them to adhere slightly to the spoon when hot. All *purées* should be somewhat thicker.

## STOCK, White (to be used in the preparation of White Soups).

*Ingredients.*—4 lbs. of knuckle of veal, any poultry trimmings, 4 slices of lean ham, 3 carrots, 2 onions, 1 head of celery, 12 white peppercorns, 2 oz. of salt, 1 blade of mace, a bunch of herbs, 1 oz. butter, 4 quarts of water. *Mode.*—Cut up the veal, and put it with the bones and trimmings of poultry, and the ham, into the stewpan, which has been rubbed with the butter. Moisten with ½ a pint of water, and simmer till the gravy begins to flow. Then add the 4 quarts of water and the remainder of the ingredients; simmer for 5 hours. After skimming and straining it carefully through a very fine hair sieve, it will be ready for use. *Time.*—5½ hours. *Average cost*, 9*d.* per quart.

*Note.*—When stronger stock is desired, double the quantity of veal, or put in an old fowl. The liquor in which a young turkey has been boiled, is an excellent addition to all white stock or soups.

## STOCK, Consommé or White, for many Sauces.

Consommé is made precisely in the same manner as white stock, and, for ordinary purposes, will be found quite good enough. When, however, a stronger stock is desired, either put in half the quantity of water, or double that of the meat. This is a very good foundation for all white sauces.

## STRAWBERRY JAM.

*Ingredients.*—To every lb. of fruit allow ½ pint of red-currant juice, 1¼ lb. of loaf sugar. *Mode.*—Strip the currants from the stalks, put them into a jar; place this jar in a saucepan of boiling water, and simmer until the juice is well drawn from the fruit; strain the currants, measure the juice, put it into a preserving pan, and add the sugar. Select well-ripened but sound strawberries; pick them from the stalks, and when the sugar is dissolved in the currant-juice, put in the fruit. Simmer the whole over a moderate fire, from ½ to ¾ hour, carefully removing the scum as it rises. Stir the jam only enough to prevent it from burning at the bottom of the pan, as the fruit should be preserved as whole as possible. Put the jam into jars, and when cold, cover down. *Time.*—½ to ¾ hour, reckoning from the time the jam simmers all over. *Average cost*, from 7*d.* to 8*d.* per lb. pot. *Sufficient.*—12 pints of strawberries will make 12 lbs. of jam. *Seasonable* in June and July.

## STRAWBERRY JELLY.

*Ingredients.*—Strawberries, pounded sugar; to every pint of juice allow 1¼ oz. of isinglass. *Mode.*—Pick the strawberries, put them into a pan, squeeze them well with a wooden spoon, add sufficient pounded sugar to sweeten them nicely, and let them remain for 1 hour, that the juice may be extracted; then add ½ pint of water to every pint of juice. Strain the strawberry-juice and water through a bag; measure it, and to every pint allow 1¼ oz. of isinglass, melted and clarified in ¼ pint of water. Mix this with the juice; put the jelly into a mould, and set the mould in ice. A little lemon-juice added to the strawberry-juice improves the flavour of the jelly, if the fruit is very ripe; but it must be well strained before it is put to the other ingredients, or it will make the jelly muddy. *Time.*—1 hour to draw the juice. *Average cost*, with the best isinglass, 3*s.* *Sufficient.*—Allow 1½ pint of jelly for 5 or 6 persons. *Seasonable* in June, July, and August.

## STRAWBERRIES and CREAM.

*Ingredients.*—To every pint of picked strawberries allow 1/3 pint of cream, 2 oz. of finely-pounded sugar. *Mode.*—Pick the stalks from the fruit, place it on a glass dish, sprinkle over it pounded sugar, and slightly stir the strawberries, that they may all be equally sweetened; pour the cream over the top, and serve. Devonshire cream, when it can be obtained, is exceedingly delicious for this dish; and, if very thick indeed, may be diluted with a little thin cream or milk. *Average cost* for this quantity, with cream at 1*s.* per pint, 1*s.* *Sufficient* for 2 persons. *Seasonable* in June and July.

## STRAWBERRIES, Preserved in Wine.

*Ingredients.*—To every quart bottle allow ¼ lb. of finely-pounded loaf sugar; sherry or Madeira. *Mode.*—Let the fruit be gathered in fine weather, and used as soon as picked. Have ready some perfectly dry glass bottles, and some nice soft corks or bungs. Pick the stalks from the strawberries, drop them into the bottles, sprinkling amongst them pounded sugar in the above proportion, and when the fruit reaches to the neck of the bottle, fill up with sherry or Madeira. Cork the bottles down with new corks, and dip them into melted resin. *Seasonable.*—Make this in June or July.

## STRAWBERRIES, to Preserve Whole.

*Ingredients.*—To every lb. of fruit allow 1½ lb. of good loaf sugar, 1 pint of red-currant juice. *Mode.*—Choose the strawberries not too ripe, of a fine large sort and of a good colour. Pick off the stalks, lay the strawberries in a dish, and sprinkle over them half the quantity of sugar, which must be finely pounded. Shake the dish gently, that the sugar may be equally distributed and touch the under-side of the fruit, and let it remain for 1 day. Then have ready the currant-juice, drawn as for red-currant jelly; boil it with the remainder of the sugar until it forms a thin syrup, and in this simmer the strawberries and sugar, until the whole is sufficiently jellied. Great care must be taken not to stir the fruit roughly, as it should be preserved as whole as possible. Strawberries prepared in this manner are very good served in glasses and mixed with thin cream. *Time.*—¼ hour to 20 minutes to simmer the strawberries in the syrup. *Seasonable* in June and July.

**OPEN TART.**

## STRAWBERRY, Open Tart of, or any other Kind of Preserve.

*Ingredients.*—Trimmings of puff-paste, any kind of jam. *Mode.*—Butter a tart-pan of the shape shown in the engraving, roll out the paste to the thickness of ½ an inch, and line the pan with it; prick a few holes at the bottom with a fork, and bake the tart in a brisk oven from 10 to 15 minutes. Let the paste cool a little; then fill it with preserve, place a few stars or leaves on it, which have been previously cut out of the paste and baked, and the tart is ready for table. By making it in this manner, both the flavour and colour of the jam are preserved, which would otherwise be lost, were it baked in the oven on the paste; and, besides, so much jam is not required. *Time.*—10 to 15 min. *Average cost,* 8*d*. *Sufficient.*—1 tart for 3 persons. *Seasonable* at any time.

**OPEN-TART MOULD.**

## STURGEON, Baked.

*Ingredients.*—1 small sturgeon, salt and pepper to taste, 1 small bunch of herbs, the juice of ½ lemon, ¼ lb. of butter, 1 pint of white wine. *Mode.*—Cleanse the fish thoroughly, skin it, and split it along the belly without separating it; have ready a large baking-dish, in which lay the fish, sprinkle over the seasoning and herbs very finely minced, and moisten it with the lemon-juice and wine. Place the butter in small pieces over the whole of the fish, put it in the oven, and baste frequently; brown it nicely, and serve with its own gravy. *Time.*—Nearly 1 hour. *Average cost*, 1s. to 1s. 6d. per lb. *Seasonable* from August to March.

## STURGEON, Roast.

*Ingredients.*—Veal stuffing, buttered paper, the tail-end of a sturgeon. *Mode.*—Cleanse the fish, bone and skin it; make a nice veal stuffing (*see* Forcemeats), and fill it with the part where the bones came from; roll it in buttered paper, bind it up firmly with tape, like a fillet of veal, and roast it in a Dutch oven before a clear fire. Serve with good brown gravy, or plain melted butter. *Time.*—About 1 hour. *Average costs*, 1s. to 1s. 6d. per lb. *Seasonable* from August to March.

*Note.*—Sturgeon maybe plainly boiled, and served with Dutch sauce. The fish is very firm, and requires long boiling.

## SUET PUDDING, to serve with Roast Meat.

*Ingredients.*—1 lb. of flour, 6 oz. of finely-chopped suet, ½ saltspoonful of salt, ½ saltspoonful of pepper, ½ pint of milk or water. *Mode.*—Chop the suet very finely, after freeing it from skin, and mix it well with the flour; add the salt and pepper (this latter ingredient may be omitted if the flavour is not liked), and make the whole into a smooth paste with the above proportion of milk or water. Tie the pudding in a floured cloth, or put it into a buttered basin, and boil from 2½ to 3 hours. To enrich it, substitute 3 beaten eggs for some of the milk or water, and increase the proportion of suet. *Time.*—2½ to 3 hours. *Average cost*, 6d. *Sufficient* for 5 or 6 persons. *Seasonable* at any time.

*Note.*—When there is a joint roasting or baking, this pudding may be boiled in a long shape, and then cut into slices a few minutes before dinner is served; these slices should be laid in the dripping-pan for a minute or two, and then browned before the fire. Most children like this accompaniment to roast-meat.

## SUGAR, to Boil, to Caramel.

*Ingredients.*—To every lb. of lump sugar allow 1 gill of spring water. *Mode.*—Boil the sugar and water together very quickly over a clear fire, skimming it very carefully as soon as it boils. Keep it boiling until the sugar snaps when a little of it is dropped in a pan of cold water. If it remains hard, the sugar has attained the right degree; then squeeze in a little lemon-juice, and let it remain an instant on the fire. Set the pan into another of cold water, and the caramel is then ready for use. The insides of well-oiled moulds are often ornamented with this sugar, which with a fork should be spread over them in fine threads or network. A dish of light pastry, tastefully arranged, looks very pretty with this sugar spun lightly over it.

## SUPPERS.

Much may be done in the arrangement of a supper-table, at a very small expense, provided *taste* and *ingenuity* are exercised. The colours and flavours of the various dishes should contrast nicely; there should be plenty of fruit and flowers on the table, and the room should be well lighted. We have endeavoured to show how the various dishes may be placed; but of course these little matters entirely depend on the length and width of the table used, on individual taste, whether the tables are arranged round the room, whether down the centre, with a cross one at the top, or whether the supper is laid in two separate rooms, &c., &c. The garnishing of the dishes has also much to do with the appearance of a supper-table. Hams and tongues should be ornamented with cut vegetable flowers, raised pies with aspic jelly cut in dice, and all the dishes garnished sufficiently to be in good taste without looking absurd. The eye, in fact, should be as much gratified as the palate. Hot soup is now often served at suppers, but is not placed on the table. The servants fill the plates from a tureen on the buffet, and then hand them to the guests: when these plates are removed, the business of supper commences.

Where small rooms and large parties necessitate having a standing supper, many things enumerated in the following bill of fare may be placed on the buffet. Dishes for these suppers should be selected which may be eaten standing without any trouble. The following list may, perhaps, assist our readers in the arrangement of a buffet for a standing supper.

Beef, ham, and tongue-sandwiches, lobster and oyster-patties, sausage-rolls, meat-rolls, lobster-salad, dishes of fowls, the latter *all cut up*; dishes of sliced ham, sliced tongue, sliced beef, and galantine of veal; various jellies, blancmanges, and creams; custards in glasses, compôtes of fruit, tartlets of jam, and several dishes of small fancy pastry; dishes of fresh fruit, bon-bons, sweetmeats, two or three sponge-cakes, a few plates of biscuits, and the buffet ornamented with vases of fresh or artificial flowers. The above dishes are quite sufficient for a standing supper; where more are desired, a supper must then be laid and arranged in the usual manner.

## SUPPER, BILL OF FARE FOR A BALL, FOR 60 PERSONS (for Winter).

*Note.*—The length of the page will not admit of our giving the dishes as they should be placed on the table; they should be arranged with the large and high dishes down the centre, and the spaces filled up with the smaller dishes, fruit, and flowers, taking care that the flavours and colours contrast nicely, and that no two dishes of a sort come together. This bill of fare may be made to answer three or four purposes, placing a wedding cake or christening cake in the centre on a high stand, if required for either of these occasions. A few dishes of fowls, lobster salads, &c. &c., should be kept in reserve to replenish those that are most likely to be eaten first. A joint of cold roast and boiled beef should be placed on the buffet, as being something substantial for the gentlemen of the party to partake of. Besides the articles enumerated in the bill of fare, biscuits and wafers will be required, cream-and-water ices, tea, coffee, wines, liqueurs, soda-water, ginger-beer, and lemonade.

## SWEETBREADS, Baked (an Entrée).

*Ingredients.*—3 sweetbreads, egg and bread-crumbs, oiled butter, 3 slices of toast, brown gravy. *Mode.*—Choose large white sweetbreads; put them into warm water to draw out the blood, and to improve their colour; let them remain for rather more than 1 hour; then put them into boiling water, and allow them to simmer for about 10 minutes, which renders them firm. Take them up, drain them, brush over with egg, sprinkle with bread-crumbs; dip them in egg again, and then into more bread-crumbs. Drop on them a little oiled butter, and put the sweetbreads into a moderately-heated oven, and let them bake for nearly ¾ hour. Make 3 pieces of toast; place the sweetbreads on the toast, and pour round, but not over them, a good brown gravy. *Time.*—To soak 1 hour, to be boiled 10 minutes, baked 40 minutes. *Average cost*, 1s. to 5s. *Sufficient* for an entrée. *Seasonable.*—In full season from May to August.

**SWEETBREADS.**

## SWEETBREADS, Fried (à la Maître d'Hôtel), an Entrée.

*Ingredients.*—3 sweetbreads, egg and bread-crumbs, ¼ lb. of butter, salt and pepper to taste, rather more than ½ pint of maître-d'hôtel sauce. *Mode.*—Soak the sweetbreads in warm water for an hour; then boil them for 10 minutes; cut them in slices, egg and bread-crumb them, season with pepper and salt, and put them into a frying-pan, with the above proportion of butter. Keep turning them until done, which will be in about 10 minutes; dish them, and pour over them a maître-d'hôtel sauce. The dish may be garnished with slices of cut lemon. *Time.*—To soak 1 hour, to be boiled 10 minutes, to be fried about 10 minutes. *Average cost,* 1s. to 5s., according to the season. *Sufficient* for an entrée. *Seasonable.*—In full season from May to August.

*Note.*—The egg and bread-crumb may be omitted, and the slices of sweetbread dredged with a little flour instead, and a good gravy may be substituted for the maître-d'hôtel sauce. This is a very simple method of dressing them.

## SWEETBREADS, Stewed (an Entrée).

*Ingredients.*—3 sweetbreads, 1 pint of white stock, thickening of butter and flour, 6 tablespoonfuls of cream, 1 tablespoonful of lemon-juice, 1 blade of pounded mace, white pepper and salt to taste. *Mode.*—Soak the sweetbreads in warm water for 1 hour, and boil them for 10 minutes; take them out, put them into cold water for a few minutes; lay them in a stewpan with the stock, and simmer them gently for rather more than ½ hour. Dish them; thicken the gravy with a little butter and flour; let it boil up, add the remaining ingredients, allow the sauce to get quite *hot*, but *not boil*, and pour it over the sweetbreads. *Time.*—To soak 1 hour, to be boiled 10 minutes, stewed rather more than ½ hour. *Average cost*, from 1s. to 5s., according to the season. *Sufficient* for an entrée. *Seasonable.*—In full season from May to August.

*Note.*—A few mushrooms added to this dish, and stewed with the sweetbreads, will be found an improvement.

## SWEETBREADS, Lambs', larded, and Asparagus (an Entrée).

*Ingredients.*—2 or 3 sweetbreads, ½ pint of veal stock, white pepper and salt to taste, a small bunch of green onions, 1 blade of pounded mace, thickening of butter and flour, 2 eggs, nearly ½ pint of cream, 1 teaspoonful of minced parsley, a very little grated nutmeg. *Mode.*—Soak the sweetbreads in lukewarm water, and put them into a saucepan with sufficient boiling water to cover them, and let them simmer for 10 minutes; then take them out and put them into cold water. Now lard them, lay them in a stewpan, add the stock, seasoning, onions, mace, and a thickening of butter and flour, and stew gently for ¼ hour or 20 minutes. Beat up the egg with the cream, to which add the minced parsley and a very little grated nutmeg. Put this to the other ingredients; stir it well till quite hot, but do not let it boil after the cream is added, or it will curdle. Have ready some asparagus-tops, boiled; add these to the sweetbreads, and serve. *Time.*—Altogether ½ hour. *Average cost*, 2*s.* 6*d.* to 3*s.* 6*d.* each. *Sufficient.*—3 sweetbreads for 1 entrée. *Seasonable* from Easter to Michaelmas.

## SWEETBREADS, another Way to Dress (an Entrée).

*Ingredients.*—Sweetbreads, egg and bread-crumbs, ½ pint of gravy, ½ glass of sherry. *Mode.*—Soak the sweetbreads in water for an hour, and throw them into boiling water to render them firm. Let them stew gently for about ¼ hour, take them out and put them into a cloth to drain all the water from them. Brush them over with egg, sprinkle them with bread-crumbs, and either brown them in the oven or before the fire. Have ready the above quantity of gravy, to which add ½ glass of sherry; dish the sweetbreads, pour the gravy under them, and garnish with water-cresses. *Time.*—Rather more than ½ hour. *Average cost*, 2*s.* 6*d.* to 3*s.* 6*d.* each. *Sufficient*—3 sweetbreads for 1 entrée. *Seasonable*, from Easter to Michaelmas.

## SYLLABUB.

*Ingredients.*—1 pint of sherry or white wine, ½ grated nutmeg, sugar to taste, 1½ pint of milk. *Mode.*—Put the wine into a bowl, with the grated nutmeg and plenty of pounded sugar, and milk into it the above proportion of milk from the cow. Clouted cream may be laid on the top, with pounded cinnamon or nutmeg and sugar; and a little brandy may be added to the wine before the milk is put in. In some counties, cider is substituted for the wine: when this is used, brandy must always be added. Warm milk may be poured on from a spouted jug or teapot; but it must be held very high. *Average cost*, 2*s*. *Sufficient* for 5 or 6 persons. *Seasonable* at any time.

## SYLLABUBS, Whipped.

*Ingredients.*—½ pint of cream, ¼ pint of sherry, half that quantity of brandy, the juice of ½ lemon, a little grated nutmeg, 3 oz. of pounded sugar, whipped cream the same as for trifle. *Mode.*—Mix all the ingredients together, put the syllabub into glasses, and over the top of them heap a little whipped cream, made in the same manner as for trifle. Solid syllabub is made by whisking or milling the mixture to a stiff froth, and putting it in the glasses, without the whipped cream at the top. *Average cost*, 1*s*. 8*d*. *Sufficient* to fill 8 or 9 glasses. *Seasonable* at any time.

## SYRUP for Jellies, to Clarify.

*Ingredients.*—To every quart of water allow 2 lbs. of loaf sugar; the white of 1 egg. *Mode.*—Put the sugar and water into a stewpan; set it on the fire, and, when the sugar is dissolved, add the white of the egg, whipped up with a little water. Whisk the whole well together, and simmer very gently until it has thrown up all the scum. Take this off as it rises, strain the syrup through a fine sieve or cloth into a basin, and keep it for use.

## TAPIOCA PUDDING.

*Ingredients.*—3 oz. of tapioca, 1 quart of milk, 2 oz. of butter, ¼ lb. of sugar, 4 eggs, flavouring of vanilla, grated lemon-rind, or bitter almonds. *Mode.*—Wash the tapioca, and let it stew gently in the milk by the side of the fire for ¼ hour, occasionally stirring it; then let it cool a little; mix with it the butter, sugar, and eggs, which should be wall beaten, and flavour with either of the above ingredients, putting in about 12 drops of the essence of almonds or vanilla, whichever is preferred. Butter a pie-dish, and line the edges with puff-paste; put in the pudding, and bake in a moderate oven for an hour. If the pudding is boiled, add a little more tapioca, and boil it in a buttered basin 1½ hour. *Time.*—1 hour to bake, 1½ hour to boil. *Average cost*, 1*s.* 2*d. Sufficient* for 5 or 6 persons. *Seasonable* at any time.

## TAPIOCA SOUP.

*Ingredients.*—5 oz. of tapioca, 2 quarts of stock. *Mode.*—Put the tapioca into cold stock, and bring it gradually to a boil. Simmer gently till tender, and serve. *Time.*—Rather more than 1 hour. *Average cost*, 1*s.* 6*d.* per quart. *Seasonable* all the year. *Sufficient* for 8 persons.

## TARTLETS.

*Ingredients.*—Trimmings of puff-paste, any jam or marmalade that may be preferred. *Mode.*—Roll out the paste to the thickness of about ½ inch; butter some small round patty-pans, line them with it, and cut off the superfluous paste close to the edge of the pan. Put a small piece of bread into each tartlet (this is to keep them in shape), and bake in a brisk oven for about 10 minutes, or rather longer. When they are done, and are of a nice colour, take the pieces of bread out carefully, and replace them by a spoonful of jam or marmalade. Dish them high on a white d'oyley, piled high in the centre, and serve. *Time.*—10 to 15 minutes. *Average cost*, 1*d.* each. *Sufficient.*—1 lb. of paste will make 2 dishes of tartlets. *Seasonable* at any time.

**DISH OF TARTLETS.**

## TARTLETS, Polish.

*Ingredients.*—Puff-paste, the white of an egg, pounded sugar. *Mode.*—Roll some good puff-paste out thin, and cut it into 2½-inch squares; brush each square over with the white of an egg, then fold down the corners, so that they all meet in the middle of each piece of paste; slightly press the two pieces together, brush them over with the egg, sift over sugar, and bake in a nice quick oven for about ¼ hour. When they are done, make a little hole in the middle of the paste, and fill it up with apricot jam, marmalade, or red-currant jelly. Pile them high in the centre of a dish, on a napkin, and garnish with the same preserve the tartlets are filled with. *Time.*—¼ hour or 20 minutes. *Average cost,* with ½ lb. of puff-paste, 1*s*. *Sufficient* for 2 dishes of pastry. *Seasonable* at any time.

*Note.*—It should be borne in mind, that, for all dishes of small pastry, such as the preceding, trimmings of puff-paste, left from larger tarts, answer as well as making the paste expressly.

## TEA, to make.

There is very little art in making good tea; if the water is boiling, and there is no sparing of the fragrant leaf, the beverage will almost invariably be good. The old-fashioned plan of allowing a teaspoonful to each person, and one over, is still practised. Warm the teapot with boiling water; let it remain for two or three minutes for the vessel to become thoroughly hot, then pour it away. Put in the tea, pour in from ½ to ¾ pint of *boiling* water, close the lid, and let it stand for the tea to draw from 5 to 10 minutes; then fill up the pot with water. The tea will be quite spoiled unless made with water that is actually *boiling,* as the leaves will not open, and the flavour not be extracted from them; the beverage will consequently be colourless and tasteless,—in fact, nothing but tepid water. Where there is a very large party to make tea for, it is a good plan to have two teapots, instead of putting a large quantity of tea into one pot; the tea, besides, will go farther. When the infusion has been once completed, the addition of fresh tea adds very little to the strength; so, when more is required, have the pot emptied of the old leaves, scalded, and fresh tea made in the usual manner. Economists say that a few grains of carbonate of soda, added before the boiling water is poured on the tea, assist to draw out the goodness; if the water is very hard, perhaps it is a good plan, as the soda softens it; but care must be taken to use this ingredient sparingly, as it is liable to give the tea a soapy taste if added in too large a quantity. For mixed tea, the usual proportion is four spoonfuls of black to one of green; more of the latter when the flavour is very much liked; but strong green tea is highly pernicious, and should never be partaken of too freely. *Time.*—2 minutes to warm the teapot, 5 to 10 minutes to draw the strength from the tea. *Sufficient.*—Allow 1 teaspoonful to each person.

## TEA-CAKES.

*Ingredients.*—2 lbs. of flour, ½ teaspoonful of salt, ¼ lb. of butter or lard, 1 egg, a piece of German yeast the size of a walnut, warm milk. *Mode.*—Put the flour (which should be perfectly dry) into a basin; mix with it the salt, and rub in the butter or lard; then beat the egg well, stir to it the yeast, and add these to the flour with as much warm milk as will make the whole into a smooth paste, and knead it well. Let it rise near the fire, and, when well risen, form it into cakes; place them on tins, let them rise again for a few minutes before putting them into the oven, and bake from ¼ to ½ hour in a moderate oven. These are very nice with a few currants and a little sugar added to the other ingredients, they should be put in after the butter is rubbed in. These cakes should be buttered, and eaten hot as soon as baked; but, when stale, they are very nice split and toasted; or, if dipped in milk, or even water, and covered with a basin in the oven till hot, they will be almost equal to new. *Time.*—¼ to ½ hour. *Average cost*, 10*d*. *Sufficient* to make 8 tea-cakes. *Seasonable* at any time.

## TEA-CAKES, to toast.

Cut each tea-cake into three or four slices, according to its thickness; toast them on both sides before a nice clear fire, and as each slice is done, spread it with butter on both sides. When a cake is toasted, pile the slices one on the top of the other, cut them into quarters, put them on a very hot plate, and send the cakes immediately to table. As they are wanted, send them in hot, one or two at a time, as, if allowed to stand, they spoil, unless kept in a muffin-plate over a basin of boiling water.

TEA-CAKES.

## TEAL, Roast.

*Ingredients.*—Teal, butter, a little flour. *Mode.*—Choose fat, plump birds, after the frost has set in, as they are generally better flavoured; truss them in the same manner as wild duck; roast them before a brisk fire, and keep them well basted. Serve with brown or orange gravy, water-cresses, and a cut lemon. The remains of teal make excellent hash. *Time.*—From 9 to 15 minutes. *Average cost*, 1s. each; but seldom bought. *Sufficient.*—2 for a dish. *Seasonable* from October to February.

## TEAL.

TEAL, being of the same character as widgeon and wild duck, may be treated, in carving, in the same style.

## TENCH, Matelot of.

*Ingredients.*—½ pint of stock, ½ pint of port wine, 1 dozen button onions, a few mushrooms, a faggot of herbs, 2 blades of mace, 1 oz. of butter, 1 teaspoonful of minced parsley, thyme, 1 shalot, 2 anchovies, 1 teacupful of stock, flour, 1 dozen oysters, the juice of ½ lemon; the number of tench, according to size. *Mode.*—Scale and clean the tench, cut them into pieces, and lay them in a stewpan; add the stock, wine, onions, mushrooms, herbs, and mace, and simmer gently for ½ hour. Put into another stewpan all the remaining ingredients but the oysters and lemon-juice, and boil slowly for 10 minutes, when add the strained liquor from the tench, and keep stirring it over the fire until somewhat reduced. Rub it through a sieve, pour it over the tench with the oysters, which must be previously scalded in their own liquor, squeeze in the lemon-juice, and serve. Garnish with croûtons. *Time.*—¾ hour. *Seasonable* from October to June.

## TENCH, Stewed with Wine.

*Ingredients.*—½ pint of stock, ½ pint of Madeira or sherry, salt and pepper to taste, 1 bay-leaf, thickening of butter and flour. *Mode.*—Clean and crimp the tench, carefully lay it in a stewpan with the stock, wine, salt and pepper, and bay-leaf, let it stew gently for ½ hour; then take it out, put it on a dish, and keep hot. Strain the liquor, and thicken it with butter and flour kneaded together, and stew for 5 minutes. If not perfectly smooth, squeeze it through a tammy, add a very little cayenne, and pour over the fish. Garnish with balls of veal forcemeat. *Time.*—Rather more than ½ hour. *Seasonable* from October to June.

## TENDRONS DE VEAU, Stewed (an Entrée).

*Ingredients.*—The gristles from 2 breasts of veal, white stock, 1 faggot of savoury herbs, 2 blades of pounded mace, 4 cloves, 2 carrots, 2 onions, a strip of lemon-peel. *Mode.*—The *tendrons* or gristles, which are found round the front of a breast of veal, are now very frequently served as an entrée, and when well dressed, make a nice and favourite dish. Detach the gristles from the bone, and cut them neatly out, so as not to spoil the joint for roasting or stewing. Put them into a stewpan, with sufficient stock to cover them; add the herbs, mace, cloves, carrots, onions, and lemon, and simmer these for nearly, or quite, 4 hours. They should be stewed until a fork will enter the meat easily. Take them up, drain them, strain the gravy, boil it down to a glaze, with which glaze the meat. Dish the *tendrons* in a circle with croûtons fried of a nice colour placed between each; and put mushroom sauce, or a purée of green peas or tomatoes, in the middle. *Time.*—4 hours. *Sufficient* for 1 entrée. *Seasonable.*—With peas, from June to August.

## TENDRONS DE VEAU (an Entrée).

*Ingredients.*—The gristles from 2 breasts of veal, white stock, 1 faggot of savoury herbs, 1 blade of pounded mace, 4 cloves, 2 carrots, 2 onions, a strip of lemon-peel, egg and bread-crumbs, 2 tablespoonfuls of chopped mushrooms, salt and pepper to taste, 2 tablespoonfuls of sherry, the yolk of 1 egg, 3 tablespoonfuls of cream. *Mode.*—After removing the gristles from a breast of veal, stew them for 4 hours, as in the preceding recipe, with stock, herbs, mace, cloves, carrots, onions, and lemon-peel. When perfectly tender, lift them out and remove any bones or hard parts remaining. Put them between two dishes, with a weight on the top, and when cold, cut them into slices. Brush these over with egg, sprinkle with bread-crumbs, and fry a pale brown. Take ½ pint of the gravy they were boiled in, add 2 tablespoonfuls of chopped mushrooms, a seasoning of salt and pepper, the sherry, and the yolk of an egg beaten with 3 tablespoonfuls of cream. Stir the sauce over the fire until it thickens; when it is on the *point of boiling*, dish the tendrons in a circle, and pour the sauce in the middle. Tendrons are dressed in a variety of ways,—with sauce à l'Espagnole, vegetables of all kinds: when they are served with a purée, they should always be glazed. *Time.*—4½ hours. *Average cost.*—Usually bought with breast of veal. *Sufficient* for an entrée. *Seasonable* from March to October.

## TETE DE VEAU EN TORTUE (an Entrée).

*Ingredients.*—Half a calf's head, or the remains of a cold boiled one; rather more than 1 pint of good white stock, 1 glass of sherry or Madeira, cayenne and salt to taste, about 12 mushroom-buttons (when obtainable), 6 hard-boiled eggs, 4 gherkins, 8 quenelles, or forcemeat balls, 12 crayfish, 12 croûtons. *Mode.*—Half a calf's head is sufficient to make a good entrée, and if there are any remains of a cold one left from the preceding day, it will answer very well for this dish. After boiling the head until tender, remove the bones, and cut the meat into neat pieces; put the stock into a stewpan, add the wine, and a seasoning of salt and cayenne; fry the mushrooms in butter for 2 or 3 minutes, and add these to the gravy. Boil this quickly until somewhat reduced; then put in the yolks of the hard-boiled eggs *whole*, and the whites cut in small pieces, and the gherkins chopped. Have ready a few veal quenelles, add these, with the slices of head, to the other ingredients, and let the whole get thoroughly hot, *without boiling*. Arrange the pieces of head as high in the centre of the dish as possible; pour over them the ragoût, and garnish with the crayfish and croûtons placed alternately. A little of the gravy should also be served in a tureen. *Time.*—About ½ hour to reduce the stock. *Sufficient* for 6 or 7 persons. *Average cost,* exclusive of the calf's head, 2*s.* 9*d. Seasonable* from March to October.

## TIPSY CAKE.

**TIPSY CAKE.**

*Ingredients.*—1 moulded sponge or Savoy cake, sufficient sweet wine or sherry to soak it, 6 tablespoonfuls of brandy, 2 oz. of sweet almonds, 1 pint of rich custard. *Mode.*—Procure a cake that is three or four days old,—either sponge, Savoy, or rice answering for the purpose of a tipsy cake. Cut the bottom of the cake level, to make it stand firm in the dish; make a small hole in the centre, and pour in and over the cake sufficient sweet wine or sherry, mixed with the above proportion of brandy, to soak it nicely. When the cake is well soaked, blanch and cut the almonds into strips, stick them all over the cake, and pour round it a good custard, made by our recipe, allowing 8 eggs instead of 5 to the pint of milk. The cakes are sometimes crumbled and soaked, and a whipped cream heaped over them, the same as for trifles. *Time.*—About 2 hours to soak the cake. *Average cost*, 4s. 6d. *Sufficient* for 1 dish. *Seasonable* at any time.

## TIPSY CAKE, an easy way of making.

*Ingredients.*—12 stale small sponge-cakes, raisin wine, ½ lb. of jam, 1 pint of custard (*see* Custard). *Mode.*—Soak the sponge-cakes, which should be stale (on this account they should be cheaper), in a little raisin wine; arrange them on a deep glass dish in four layers, putting a layer of jam between each, and pour round them a pint of custard, made by recipe, decorating the top with cut preserved-fruit. *Time.*—2 hours to soak the cakes. *Average cost*, 2s. 6d. *Sufficient* for 1 dish. *Seasonable* at any time.

## TOAD-IN-THE-HOLE (Cold Meat Cookery).

*Ingredients.*—6 oz. of flour, 1 pint of milk, 3 eggs, butter, a few slices of cold mutton, pepper and salt to taste, 2 kidneys. *Mode.*—Make a smooth batter of flour, milk, and eggs in the above proportion; butter a baking-dish, and pour in the batter. Into this place a few slices of cold mutton, previously well seasoned, and the kidneys, which should be cut into rather small pieces; bake about 1 hour, or rather longer, and send it to table in the dish it was baked in. Oysters or mushrooms may be substituted for the kidneys, and will be found exceedingly good. *Time.*—Rather more than 1 hour. *Average cost*, exclusive of the cold meat, 8*d*. *Seasonable* at any time.

## TOAD-IN-THE-HOLE (a Homely but Savoury Dish).

*Ingredients.*—1½ lb. of rump-steak, 1 sheep's kidney, pepper and salt to taste. For the batter, 3 eggs, 1 pint of milk, 4 tablespoonfuls of flour, ½ saltspoonful of salt. *Mode.*—Cut up the steak and kidney into convenient-sized pieces, and put them into a pie-dish, with a good seasoning of salt and pepper; mix the flour with a small quantity of milk at first, to prevent its being lumpy; add the remainder, and the 3 eggs, which should be well beaten; put in the salt, stir the batter for about 5 minutes, and pour it over the steak. Place it in a tolerably brisk oven immediately, and bake for 1½ hour. *Time.*—1½ hour. *Average cost*, 1*s*. 9*d*. *Sufficient* for 4 or 5 persons. *Seasonable* at any time.

*Note.*—The remains of cold beef, rather underdone, may be substituted for the steak, and, when liked, the smallest possible quantity of minced onion or shalot may be added.

## TOAST, to make Dry.

To make dry toast properly, a great deal of attention is required; much more, indeed, than people generally suppose. Never use new bread for making any kind of toast, as it eats heavy, and, besides, is very extravagant. Procure a loaf of household bread about two days old; cut off as many slices as may be required, not quite ¼ inch in thickness; trim off the crusts and ragged edges, put the bread on a toasting-fork, and hold it before a very clear fire. Move it backwards and forwards until the bread is nicely coloured; then turn it and toast the other side, and do not place it so near the fire that it blackens. Dry toast should be more gradually made than buttered toast, as its great beauty consists in its crispness, and this cannot be attained unless the process is slow and the bread is allowed gradually to colour. It should never be made long before it is wanted, as it soon becomes tough, unless placed on the fender in front of the fire. As soon as each piece is ready, it should be put into a rack, or stood upon its edges, and sent quickly to table.

## TOAST, to make Hot Buttered.

A loaf of household bread about two days old answers for making toast better than cottage bread, the latter not being a good shape, and too crusty for the purpose. Cut as many nice even slices as may be required, rather more than ¼ inch in thickness, and toast them before a very bright fire, without allowing the bread to blacken, which spoils the appearance and flavour of all toast. When of a nice colour on both sides, put it on a hot plate; divide some good butter into small pieces, place them on the toast, set this before the fire, and when the butter is just beginning to melt, spread it lightly over the toast. Trim off the crust and ragged edges, divide each round into 4 pieces, and send the toast quickly to table. Some persons cut the slices of toast across from corner to corner, so making the pieces of a three-cornered shape. Soyer recommends that each slice should be cut into pieces as soon as it is buttered, and when all are ready, that they should be piled lightly on the dish they are intended to be served on. He says that by cutting through 4 or 5 slices at a time, all the butter is squeezed out of the upper ones, while the bottom one is swimming in fat liquid. It is highly essential to use good butter for making this dish.

## TOAST-AND-WATER.

*Ingredients.*—A slice of bread, 1 quart of boiling water. *Mode.*—Cut a slice from a stale loaf (a piece of hard crust is better than anything else for the purpose), toast it of a nice brown on every side, but *do not allow it to burn or blacken*. Put it into a jug, pour the boiling water over it, cover it closely, and let it remain until cold. When strained, it will be ready for use. Toast-and-water should always be made a short time before it is required, to enable it to get cold: if drunk in a tepid or lukewarm state, it is an exceedingly disagreeable beverage. If, as is sometimes the case, this drink is wanted in a hurry, put the toasted bread into a jug, and only just cover it with the boiling water; when this is cool, cold water may be added in the proportion required, the toast-and-water strained; it will then be ready for use, and is more expeditiously prepared than by the above method.

## TOAST SANDWICHES.

*Ingredients.*—Thin cold toast, thin slices of bread-and-butter, pepper and salt to taste. *Mode.*—Place a very thin piece of cold toast between 2 slices of thin bread-and-butter in the form of a sandwich, adding a seasoning of pepper and salt. This sandwich may be varied by adding a little pulled meat, or very fine slices of cold meat, to the toast, and in any of these forms will be found very tempting to the appetite of an invalid.

## TOFFEE, Everton.

*Ingredients.*—1 lb. of powdered loaf sugar, 1 teacupful of water, ¼ lb. of butter, 6 drops of essence of lemon. *Mode.*—Put the water and sugar into a brass pan, and beat the butter to a cream. When the sugar is dissolved, add the butter, and keep stirring the mixture over the fire until it sets, when a little is poured on to a buttered dish; and just before the toffee is done, add the essence of lemon. Butter a dish or tin, pour on it the mixture, and when cool, it will easily separate from the dish. Butter-Scotch, an excellent thing for coughs, is made with brown, instead of white sugar, omitting the water, and flavoured with ½ oz. of powdered ginger. It is made in the same manner as toffee. *Time.*—18 to 35 minutes. *Average cost*, 10*d*. *Sufficient* to make a lb. of toffee.

## TOMATO SAUCE for Keeping (Excellent).

*Ingredients.*—To every quart of tomato-pulp allow 1 pint of cayenne vinegar, ¾ oz. of shalots, ¾ oz. of garlic, peeled and cut in slices; salt to taste. To every six quarts of liquor, 1 pint of soy, 1 pint of anchovy-sauce. *Mode.*—Gather the tomatoes quite ripe; bake them in a slow oven till tender; rub them through a sieve, and to every quart of pulp add cayenne vinegar, shalots, garlic, and salt, in the above proportion; boil the whole together till the garlic and shalots are quite soft; then rub it through a sieve, put it again into a saucepan, and, to every six quarts of the liquor, add 1 pint of soy and the same quantity of anchovy-sauce, and boil altogether for about 20 minutes; bottle off for use, and carefully seal or resin the corks. This will keep good for 2 or 3 years, but will be fit for use in a week. A useful and less expensive sauce may be made by omitting the anchovy and soy. *Time.*—Altogether 1 hour. *Seasonable.*—Make this from the middle of September to the end of October.

## TOMATO SAUCE for Keeping (Excellent).

*Ingredients.*—1 dozen tomatoes, 2 teaspoonfuls of the best powdered ginger, 1 dessertspoonful of salt, 1 head of garlic chopped fine, 2 tablespoonfuls of vinegar, 1 dessertspoonful of Chili vinegar (a small quantity of cayenne may be substituted for this). *Mode.*—Choose ripe tomatoes, put them into a stone jar, and stand them in a cool oven until quite tender; when cold, take the skins and stalks from them, mix the pulp with the liquor which is in the jar, but do not strain it; add all the other ingredients, mix well together, and put it into well-sealed bottles. Stored away in a cool, dry place, it will keep good for years. It is ready for use as soon as made, but the flavour is better after a week or two. Should it not appear to keep, turn it out, and boil it up with a little additional ginger and cayenne. For immediate use, the skins should be put into a wide-mouthed bottle with a little of the different ingredients, and they will be found very nice for hashes or stews. *Time.*—4 or 5 hours in a *cool* oven. *Seasonable* from the middle of September to the end of October.

## TOMATO SAUCE for Keeping (Excellent).

*Ingredients.*—3 dozen tomatoes; to every pound of tomato-pulp allow 1 pint of Chili vinegar, 1 oz. of garlic, 1 oz. of shalot, 2 oz. of salt, 1 large green capsicum, ½ teaspoonful of cayenne, 2 pickled gherkins, 6 pickled onions, 1 pint of common vinegar, and the juice of 6 lemons. *Mode.*— Choose the tomatoes when quite ripe and red; put them in a jar with a cover to it, and bake them till tender. The better way is to put them in the oven overnight, when it will not be too hot, and examine them in the morning to see if they are tender. Do not allow them to remain in the oven long enough to break them; but they should be sufficiently soft to skin nicely and rub through the sieve. Measure the pulp, and to each pound of pulp add the above proportion of vinegar and other ingredients, taking care to chop very fine the garlic, shalot, capsicum, onion, and gherkins. Boil the whole together till everything is tender; then again rub it through a sieve, and add the lemon-juice. Now boil the whole again till it becomes as thick as cream, and keep continually stirring; bottle it when quite cold, cork well, and seal the corks. If the flavour of garlic and shalot is very much disliked, diminish the quantities. *Time.*—Bake the tomatoes in a *cool* oven all night. *Seasonable* from the middle of September to the end of October.

*Note.*—A quantity of liquor will flow from the tomatoes, which must be put through the sieve with the rest. Keep it well stirred whilst on the fire, and use a wooden spoon.

## TOMATO SAUCE, Hot, to serve with Cutlets, Roast Meats, &c.

*Ingredients.*—6 tomatoes, 2 shalots, 1 clove, 1 blade of mace, salt and cayenne to taste, ¼ pint of gravy or stock. *Mode.*—Cut the tomatoes in two, and squeeze the juice and seeds out; put them in a stewpan with all the ingredients, and let them simmer *gently* until the tomatoes are tender enough to pulp; rub the whole through a sieve, boil it for a few minutes, and serve. The shalots and spices may be omitted when their flavour is objected to. *Time.*—1 hour, or rather more, to simmer the tomatoes. *Average cost*, for this quantity, 1*s*. *In full season* in September and October.

## TOMATOES, Baked (Excellent).

*Ingredients.*—8 or 10 tomatoes, pepper and salt to taste, 2 oz. of butter, bread-crumbs. *Mode.*—Take off the stalks from the tomatoes; cut them into thick slices, and put them into a deep baking-dish; add a plentiful seasoning of pepper and salt, and butter in the above proportion; cover the whole with bread-crumbs; drop over these a little clarified butter; bake in a moderate oven from 20 minutes to ½ hour, and serve very hot. This vegetable dressed as above, is an exceedingly nice accompaniment to all kinds of roast meat. The tomatoes, instead of being cut in slices, may be baked whole; but they will take rather longer time to cook. *Time.*—20 minutes to ½ hour. *Average cost*, in full season, 9*d*. per basket. *Sufficient* for 5 or 6 persons. *Seasonable* in August, September, and October; but may be had, forced, much earlier.

## TOMATOES, Baked (another Mode).

*Ingredients.*—Some bread-crumbs, a little butter, onion, cayenne, and salt. *Mode.*—Bake the tomatoes whole, then scoop out a small hole at the top; fry the bread-crumbs, onion, &c., and fill the holes with this as high up as possible; then brown the tomatoes with a salamander, or in an oven, and take care that the skin does not break.

## TOMATOES, Stewed.

*Ingredients.*—8 tomatoes, pepper and salt to taste, 2 oz. of butter, 2 tablespoonfuls of vinegar. *Mode.*—Slice the tomatoes into a *lined* saucepan; season them with pepper and salt, and place small pieces of butter on them. Cover the lid down closely, and stew from 20 to 25 minutes, or until the tomatoes are perfectly tender; add the vinegar, stir two or three times, and serve with any kind of roast meat, with which they will be found a delicious accompaniment. *Time.*—20 to 25 minutes. *Average cost*, in full season, 9*d.* per basket. *Sufficient* for 4 or 5 persons. *Seasonable* from August to October; but may be had, forced, much earlier.

**STEWED TOMATOES.**

## TOMATOES, Stewed.

*Ingredients.*—8 tomatoes, about ½ pint of good gravy, thickening of butter and flour, cayenne and salt to taste. *Mode.*—Take out the stalks of the tomatoes; put them into a wide stewpan, pour over them the above proportion of good brown gravy, and stew gently until they are tender, occasionally *carefully* turning them, that they may be equally done. Thicken the gravy with a little butter and flour worked together on a plate; let it just boil up after the thickening is added, and serve. If it be at hand, these should be served on a silver or plated vegetable-dish. *Time.*—20 to 25 minutes, very gentle stewing. *Average cost*, in full season, 9*d.* per basket. *Sufficient* for 4 or 5 persons. *Seasonable* in August, September, and October; but may be had, forced, much earlier.

## TONGUE, Boiled.

*Ingredients.*—1 tongue, a bunch of savoury herbs, water. *Mode.*—In choosing a tongue, ascertain how long it has been dried or pickled, and select one with a smooth skin, which denotes its being young and tender. If a dried one, and rather hard, soak it at least for 12 hours previous to cooking it; if, however, it is fresh from the pickle, 2 or 3 hours will be sufficient for it to remain in soak. Put the tongue into a stewpan with plenty of cold water and a bunch of savoury herbs; let it gradually come to a boil, skim well, and simmer very gently until tender. Peel off the skin, garnish with tufts of cauliflowers or Brussels sprouts, and serve. Boiled tongue is frequently sent to table with boiled poultry, instead of ham, and is, by many persons, preferred. If to serve cold, peel it, fasten it down to a piece of board by sticking a fork through the root, and another through the top, to straighten it. When cold, glaze it, and put a paper ruche round the root, and garnish with tufts of parsley. *Time.*—A large smoked tongue, 4 to 4½ hours; a small one, 2½ to 3 hours. A large unsmoked tongue, 3 to 3½ hours; a small one, 2 to 2½ hours. *Average cost*, for a moderate-sized tongue, 3*s.* 6*d. Seasonable* at any time.

## TONGUES, to Cure.

*Ingredients.*—For a tongue of 7 lbs., 1 oz. of saltpetre, ½ oz. of black pepper, 4 oz. of sugar, 3 oz. of juniper berries, 6 oz. of salt. *Mode.*—Rub the above ingredients well into the tongue, and let it remain in the pickle for 10 days or a fortnight; then drain it, tie it up in brown paper, and have it smoked for about 20 days over a wood fire; or it may be boiled out of this pickle. *Time.*—From 10 to 14 days to remain in the pickle; to be smoked 24 days. *Average cost,* for a medium-sized uncured tongue, 2*s.* 6*d. Seasonable* at any time.

*Note.*—If not wanted immediately, the tongue will keep 3 or 4 weeks without being too salt; then it must not be rubbed, but only turned in the pickle.

## TONGUES, to Cure.

*Ingredients.*—9 lbs. of salt, 8 oz. of sugar, 9 oz. of powdered saltpetre. *Mode.*—Rub the above ingredients well into the tongues, and keep them in this curing mixture for 2 months, turning them every day. Drain them from the pickle, cover with brown paper, and have them smoked for about 3 weeks. *Time.*—The tongues to remain in pickle 2 months; to be smoked 3 weeks. *Sufficient.*—The above quantity of brine sufficient for 12 tongues, of 5 lbs. each. *Seasonable* at any time.

## TONGUE, to Pickle and Dress a, to Eat Cold.

*Ingredients.*—6 oz. of salt, 2 oz. of bay-salt, 1 oz. of saltpetre, 3 oz. of coarse sugar; cloves, mace, and allspice to taste; butter, common crust of flour and water. *Mode.*—Lay the tongue for a fortnight in the above pickle, turn it every day, and be particular that the spices are well pounded; put it into a small pan just large enough to hold it, place some pieces of butter on it, and cover with a common crust. Bake in a slow oven until so tender that a straw would penetrate it; take off the skin, fasten it down to a piece of board by running a fork through the root, and another through the tip, at the same time straightening it and putting it into shape. When cold, glaze it, put a paper ruche round the root, which is generally very unsightly, and garnish with tufts of parsley. *Time.*—From 3 to 4 hours in a slow oven, according to size. *Average cost*, for a medium-sized uncured tongue, 2*s*. 6*d*. *Seasonable* at any time.

## TREACLE PUDDING, Rolled.

*Ingredients.*—1 lb. of suet crust, ¼ lb. of treacle, ½ teaspoonful of grated ginger. *Mode.*—Make, with 1 lb. of flour, a suet crust by our given recipe, roll it out to the thickness of ½ inch, and spread the treacle equally over it, leaving a small margin where the paste joins; close the ends securely, tie the pudding in a floured cloth, plunge it into boiling water, and boil for 2 hours. We have inserted this pudding, being economical, and a favourite one with children; it is, of course, only suitable for a nursery, or very plain family dinner. Made with a lard instead of a suet crust, it would be very nice baked, and would be sufficiently done in from 1½ to 2 hours. *Time.*—Boiled pudding, 2 hours; baked pudding, 1½ to 2 hours. *Average cost*, 7*d*. *Sufficient* for 5 or 6 persons. *Seasonable* at any time.

## TRIFLE, to make a.

**TRIFLE.**

*Ingredients.*—For the whip, 1 pint of cream, 3 oz. of pounded sugar, the white of 2 eggs, a small glass of sherry or raisin wine. For the trifle, 1 pint of custard, made with 8 eggs to a pint of milk; 6 small sponge-cakes, or 6 slices of sponge-cake; 12 macaroons, 2 dozen ratafias, 2 oz. of sweet almonds, the grated rind of 1 lemon, a layer of raspberry or strawberry jam, ½ pint of sherry or sweet wine, 6 tablespoonfuls of brandy.

*Mode.*—The whip to lay over the top of the trifle should be made the day before it is required for table, as the flavour is better, and it is much more solid than when prepared the same day. Put into a large bowl the pounded sugar, the whites of the eggs, which should be beaten to a stiff froth, a glass of sherry or sweet wine, and the cream. Whisk these ingredients well in a cool place, and take off the froth with a skimmer as fast as it rises, and put it on a sieve to drain; continue the whisking till there is sufficient of the whip, which must be put away in a cool place to drain. The next day, place the sponge-cakes, macaroons, and ratafias at the bottom of a trifle-dish; pour over them ½ pint of sherry or sweet wine, mixed with 6 tablespoonfuls of brandy, and, should this proportion of wine not be found quite sufficient, add a little more, as the cakes should be well soaked. Over the cakes pat the grated lemon-rind, the sweet almonds, blanched and cut into strips, and a layer of raspberry or strawberry jam. Make a good custard, by recipe, using 8 instead of 5 eggs to the pint of milk, and let this cool a little; then pour it over the cakes, &c. The whip being made the day previously, and the trifle prepared, there remains nothing to do now but heap the whip lightly over the top: this should stand as high as possible, and it may be garnished with strips of bright currant jelly (see illustration), crystallized sweetmeats, or flowers; the small coloured comfits are sometimes used for the purpose of garnishing a trifle, but they are now considered rather old-fashioned. *Average cost*, with cream at 1*s.* per pint, 5*s.* 6*d*. *Sufficient* for 1 trifle. *Seasonable* at any time.

## TRIFLE, Indian.

*Ingredients.*—1 quart of milk, the rind of ½ large lemon, sugar to taste, 5 heaped tablespoonfuls of rice-flour, 1 oz. of sweet almonds, ½ pint of custard.

*Mode.*—Boil the milk and lemon-rind together until the former is well flavoured; take out the lemon-rind and stir in the rice-flour, which should first be moistened with cold milk, and add sufficient loaf sugar to sweeten it nicely. Boil gently for about 5 minutes, and keep the mixture stirred; take it off the fire, let it cool a *little*, and pour it into a glass dish. When cold, cut the rice out in the form of a star, or any other shape that may be preferred; take out the spare rice, and fill the space with boiled custard. Blanch and cut the almonds into strips; stick them over the trifle, and garnish it with pieces of bright-coloured jelly, or preserved fruits, or candied citron. *Time.*—¼ hour to simmer the milk, 5 minutes after the rice is added. *Average cost*, 1s. *Sufficient* for 1 trifle. *Seasonable* at any time.

## TRIPE, to Dress.

*Ingredients.*—Tripe, onion sauce, milk and water. *Mode.*—Ascertain that the tripe is quite fresh, and have it cleaned and dressed. Cut away the coarsest fat, and boil it in equal proportions of milk and water for ¾ hour. Should the tripe be entirely undressed, more than double that time should be allowed for it. Have ready some onion sauce, made by our given recipe, dish the tripe, smother it with the sauce, and the remainder send to table in a tureen. *Time.*—¾ hour; for undressed tripe, from 2½ to three hours. *Average cost*, 7d. per lb. *Seasonable* at any time.

*Note.*—Tripe may be dressed in a variety of ways: it may be cut in pieces and fried in batter, stewed in gravy with mushrooms, or cut into collops, sprinkled with minced onion and savoury herbs, and fried a nice brown in clarified butter.

## TROUT, Stewed.

*Ingredients.*—2 middling-sized trout, ½ onion cut in thin slices, a little parsley, 2 cloves, 1 blade of mace, 2 bay-leaves, a little thyme, salt and pepper to taste, 1 pint of medium stock, 1 glass of port wine, thickening of butter and flour. *Mode.*—Wash the fish very clean, and wipe it quite dry. Lay it in a stewpan, with all the ingredients but the butter and flour, and simmer gently for ½ hour, or rather more, should not the fish be quite done. Take it out, strain the gravy, add the thickening, and stir it over a sharp fire for 5 minutes; pour it over the trout, and serve. *Time.*—According to size, ½ hour or more. *Average cost.*—Seldom bought. *Seasonable* from May to September, and fatter from the middle to the end of August than at any other time. *Sufficient* for 4 persons. Trout may be served with anchovy or caper sauce, baked in buttered paper, or fried whole like smelts. Trout dressed à la Genévése is extremely delicate; for this proceed the same as with salmon.

## TRUFFLES, to Dress, with Champagne.

*Ingredients.*—12 fine black truffles, a few slices of fat bacon, 1 carrot, 1 turnip, 2 onions, a bunch of savoury herbs, including parsley, 1 bay-leaf, 2 cloves, 1 blade of pounded mace, 2 glasses of champagne, ½ pint of stock. *Mode.*—Carefully select the truffles, reject those that have a musty smell, and wash them well with a brush, in cold water only, until perfectly clean. Put the bacon into a stewpan, with the truffles and the remaining ingredients; simmer these gently for an hour, and let the whole cool in the stewpan. When to be served, re-warm them, and drain them on a clean cloth; then arrange them on a delicately white napkin, that it may contrast as strongly as possible with the truffles, and serve. The trimmings of truffles are used to flavour gravies, stock, sauces, &c.; and are an excellent addition to ragoûts, made dishes of fowl, &c. *Time.*—1 hour. *Average cost.*—Not often bought in this country. *Seasonable* from November to March.

## TRUFFLES A L'ITALIENNE.

*Ingredients.*—10 truffles, 1 tablespoonful of minced parsley, 1 minced shalot, salt and pepper to taste, 2 oz. of butter, 2 tablespoonfuls of good brown gravy, the juice of ½ lemon, cayenne to taste. *Mode.*—Wash the truffles and cut them into slices about the size of a penny-piece; put them into a frying-pan, with the parsley, shalot, salt, pepper, and 1 oz. of butter; stir them over the fire, that they may all be equally done, which will be in about 10 minutes, and drain off some of the butter; then add a little more fresh butter, 2 tablespoonfuls of good gravy, the juice of ½ lemon, and a little cayenne; stir over the fire until the whole is on the point of boiling, when serve. *Time.*—Altogether, 20 minutes. *Average cost.*—Not often bought in this country. *Seasonable* from November to March.

## TRUFFLES, Italian Mode of Dressing.

*Ingredients.*—10 truffles, ¼ pint of salad-oil, pepper and salt to taste, 1 tablespoonful of minced parsley, a very little finely minced garlic, 2 blades of pounded mace, 1 tablespoonful of lemon-juice. *Mode.*—After cleansing and brushing the truffles, cut them into thin slices, and put them in a baking-dish, on a seasoning of oil, pepper, salt, parsley, garlic, and mace in the above proportion. Bake them for nearly an hour, and, just before serving, add the lemon-juice, and send them to table very hot. *Time.*—

Nearly 1 hour. *Average cost.*—Not often bought in this country. *Seasonable* from November to March.

## TRUFFLES AU NATUREL.

*Ingredients.*—Truffles, buttered paper. *Mode.*—Select some fine truffles; cleanse them, by washing them in several waters with a brush, until not a particle of sand or grit remains on them; wrap each truffle in buttered paper, and bake in a hot oven for quite an hour; take off the paper, wipe the truffles, and serve them in a hot napkin. *Time.*—1 hour. *Average cost.*—Not often bought in this country. *Seasonable* from November to March.

## TURBOT.

In choosing turbot see that it is thick, and of a yellowish white; for if of a bluish tint, it is not good. The turbot-kettle, as will be seen by our cut, is made differently from ordinary fish kettles, it being less deep, whilst it is wider, and more pointed at the sides; thus exactly answering to the shape of the fish which it is intended should be boiled in it.

**TURBOT-KETTLE.**

## TURBOT, Boiled.

*Ingredients.*—6 oz. of salt to each gallon of water. *Mode.*—Choose a middling-sized turbot; for they are invariably the most valuable: if very large, the meat will be tough and thready. Three or four hours before dressing, soak the fish in salt and water to take off the slime; then thoroughly cleanse it, and with a knife make an incision down the middle of the back, to prevent the skin of the belly from cracking. Rub it over with lemon, and be particular not to cut off the fins. Lay the fish in a very clean turbot-kettle, with sufficient cold water to cover it, and salt in the above proportion. Let it gradually come to a boil, and skim very carefully; keep it gently simmering, and on no account let it boil fast, as the fish would have a very unsightly appearance. When the meat separates easily from the bone, it is done; then take it out, let it drain well, and dish it on a hot napkin. Rub a little lobster spawn through a sieve, sprinkle it over the fish, and garnish with tufts of parsley and cut lemon. Lobster or shrimp sauce, and plain melted butter, should be sent to table with it. *Time.*—After the water boils, about ½ hour for a large turbot; middling size, about 20 minutes. *Average cost,*—large turbot, from 10*s.* to 12*s.*; middling size, from 12*s.* to 15*s. Seasonable* at any time. *Sufficient,* 1 middling-sized turbot for 8 persons.

## TURBOT, to Help.

First run the fish-slice down the thickest part of the fish lengthwise, quite through to the bone, and then cut handsome and regular slices across the fish until all the meat on the upper side is helped. When the carver has removed all the meat from the upper side of the fish, the backbone should be raised, put on one side of the dish, and the under side helped as the upper.

## TURBOT À LA CREME.

*Ingredients.*—The remains of cold turbot. For sauce, 2 oz. of butter, 4 tablespoonfuls of cream; salt, cayenne, and pounded mace to taste. *Mode.*—Clear away all skin and bone from the flesh of the turbot, which should be done when it comes from table, as it causes less waste when trimmed hot. Cut the flesh into nice square pieces, as equally as possible; put into a stewpan the butter, let it melt, and add the cream and seasoning; let it just simmer for one minute, but not boil. Lay in the fish to warm, and serve it garnished with croûtons or a paste border. *Time.*—10 minutes. *Seasonable* at any time.

*Note.*—The remains of cold salmon may be dressed in this way, and the above mixture may be served in a *vol-au-vent*.

## TURBOT, Baked Fillets of.

*Ingredients.*—The remains of cold turbot, lobster sauce left from the preceding day, egg, and bread-crumbs; cayenne and salt to taste; minced parsley, nutmeg, lemon-juice. *Mode.*—After having cleared the fish from all skin and bone, divide it into square pieces of an equal size; brush them over with egg, sprinkle with bread-crumbs mixed with a little minced parsley and seasoning. Lay the fillets in a baking-dish, with sufficient butter to baste with. Bake for ¼ hour, and do not forget to keep them well moistened with the butter. Put a little lemon-juice and grated nutmeg to the cold lobster sauce; make it hot, and pour over the fish, which must be well drained from the butter. Garnish with parsley and cut lemon. *Time.*—Altogether, ½ hour. *Seasonable* at any time.

*Note.*—Cold turbot thus warmed in the remains of lobster sauce will be found much nicer than putting the fish again in water.

## TURBOT A L'ITALIENNE, Fillets of.

*Ingredients.*—The remains of cold turbot, Italian sauce. *Mode.*—Clear the fish carefully from the bone, and take away all skin, which gives an unpleasant flavour to the sauce. Make the sauce hot, lay in the fish to warm through, but do not let it boil. Garnish with croûtons. *Time.*—5 minutes. *Seasonable* all the year.

## TURBOT, or other Large Fish, Garnish for.

Take the crumb of a stale loaf, cut it into small pyramids with flat tops, and on the top of each pyramid put rather more than a tablespoonful of white of egg beaten to a stiff froth. Over this, sprinkle finely-chopped parsley and fine raspings of a dark colour. Arrange these on the napkin round the fish, one green and one brown alternately.

## TURBOT AU GRATIN.

*Ingredients.*—Remains of cold turbot, béchamel (*see* Sauces), bread-crumbs, butter. *Mode.*—Cut the flesh of the turbot into small dice, carefully freeing it from all skin and bone. Put them into a stewpan, and moisten with 4 or 5 tablespoonfuls of béchamel. Let it get thoroughly hot, but do not allow it to boil. Spread the mixture on a dish, cover with finely-grated bread-crumbs, and place small pieces of butter over the top. Brown it in the oven, or with a salamander. *Time.*—Altogether, ½ hour. *Seasonable* at any time.

# TURKEY, Boiled.

BOILED TURKEY.

*Ingredients.*—Turkey; forcemeat. *Choosing and Trussing.*—Hen turkeys are preferable for boiling, on account of their whiteness and tenderness, and one of moderate size should be selected, as a large one is not suitable for this mode of cooking. They should not be dressed until they have been killed 3 or 4 days, as they will neither look white, nor will they be tender. Pluck the bird, carefully draw, and singe it with a piece of white paper; wash it inside and out, and wipe it thoroughly dry with a cloth. Cut off the head and neck, draw the strings or sinews of the thighs, and cut off the legs at the first joint; draw the legs into the body, fill the breast with forcemeat; run a skewer through the wing and the middle joint, of the leg, quite into the leg and wing on the opposite side; break the breastbone, and make the bird look as round and as compact as possible. *Mode.*—Put the turkey into sufficient *hot* water to cover it; let it come to a boil, then carefully remove all the scum: if this is attended to, there is no occasion to boil the bird in a floured cloth; but it should be well covered with the water. Let it simmer very gently for about 1½ hour to 1¾ hour, according to the size, and serve with either white, celery, oyster, or mushroom sauce, or parsley-and-butter, a little of which should be poured over the turkey. Boiled ham, bacon, tongue, or pickled pork, should always accompany this dish; and when oyster sauce is served, the turkey should be stuffed with oyster forcemeat. *Time.*—A small turkey, 1½ hour; a large one, 1¾ hour. *Average cost*, 5*s.* 6*d.* to 7*s.* 6*d.* each, but more expensive at Christmas, on account of the great demand. *Sufficient* for 7 or 8 persons. *Seasonable* from December to February.

# TURKEY, Croquettes of (Cold Meat Cookery).

*Ingredients.*—The remains of cold turkey; to every ½ lb. of meat allow 2 oz. of ham or bacon, 2 shalots, 1 oz. of butter, 1 tablespoonful of flour, the yolks of 2 eggs, egg and bread-crumbs. *Mode.*—The smaller pieces, that will not do for a fricassée or hash, answer very well for this dish. Mince the meat finely with ham or bacon in the above proportion; make a gravy of the bones and trimmings, well seasoning it; mince the shalots, put them into a stewpan with the butter, add the flour; mix well, then put in the mince, and about ½ pint of the gravy made from the bones. (The proportion of the butter must be increased or diminished according to the quantity of mince.) When just boiled, add the yolks of 2 eggs; put the mixture out to cool, and then shape it in a wineglass. Cover the croquettes with egg and breadcrumbs, and fry them a delicate brown. Put small pieces of parsley-stems for stalks, and serve with rolled bacon cut very thin. *Time.*—8 minutes to fry the croquettes. *Seasonable* from December to February.

## TURKEY, Fricasseed (Cold Meat Cookery).

*Ingredients.*—The remains of cold roast or boiled turkey; a strip of lemon-peel, a bunch of savoury herbs, 1 onion, pepper and salt to taste, 1 pint of water, 4 tablespoonfuls of cream, the yolk of an egg. *Mode.*—Cut some nice slices from the remains of a cold turkey, and put the bones and trimmings into a stewpan, with the lemon-peel, herbs, onion, pepper, salt, and the water; stew for an hour, strain the gravy, and lay in the pieces of turkey. When warm through, add the cream and the yolk of an egg; stir it well round, and, when getting thick, take out the pieces, lay them on a hot dish, and pour the sauce over. Garnish the fricassée with sippets of toasted bread. Celery or cucumbers, cut into small pieces, may be put into the sauce; if the former, it must be boiled first. *Time.*—1 hour to make the gravy. *Average cost,* exclusive of the cold turkey, 4*d. Seasonable* from December to February.

## TURKEY, Hashed.

*Ingredients.*—The remains of cold roast turkey, 1 onion, pepper and salt to taste, rather more than 1 pint of water, 1 carrot, 1 turnip, 1 blade of mace, a bunch of savoury herbs, 1 tablespoonful of mushroom ketchup, 1 tablespoonful of port wine, thickening of butter and flour. *Mode.*—Cut the turkey into neat joints; the best pieces reserve for the hash, the inferior joints and trimmings put into a stewpan with an onion cut in slices, pepper and salt, a carrot, turnip, mace, herbs, and water in the above proportion; simmer these for an hour, then strain the gravy, thicken it with butter and flour, flavour with ketchup and port wine, and lay in the pieces of turkey to warm through; if there is any stuffing left, put that in also, as it so much improves the flavour of the gravy. When it boils, serve, and garnish the dish with sippets of toasted bread. *Time.*—1 hour to make the gravy. *Seasonable* from December to February.

## TURKEY, Roast.

*Ingredients.*—Turkey; forcemeat. *Choosing and Trussing.*—Choose cock turkeys by their short spurs and black legs, in which case they are young; if the spurs are long, and the legs pale and rough, they are old. If the bird has been long killed, the eyes will appear sunk and the feet very dry; but, if fresh, the contrary will be the case. Middling-sized fleshy turkeys are by many persons considered superior to those of an immense growth, as they are, generally speaking, much more tender. They should never be dressed the same day they are killed; but, in cold weather, should hang at least 8 days; if the weather is mild, 4 or 5 days will be found sufficient. Carefully pluck the bird, singe it with white paper, and wipe it thoroughly with a cloth; draw it, preserve the liver and gizzard, and be particular not to break the gall-bag, as no washing will remove the bitter taste it imparts where it once touches. Wash it *inside* well, and wipe it thoroughly dry with a cloth; the *outside* merely requires nicely wiping, as we have just stated. Cut off the neck close to the back, but leave enough of the crop-skin to turn over; break the leg-bone close below the knee, draw out the strings from the thighs, and flatten the breastbone to make it look plump. Have ready a forcemeat; fill the breast with this, and, if a trussing-needle is used, sew the neck over to the back; if a needle is not at hand, a skewer will answer the purpose. Run a skewer through the pinion and thigh into the body to the pinion and thigh on the other side, and press the legs as much as possible between the breast and the side-bones, and put the liver under one pinion and the gizzard under the other. Pass a string across the back of the bird, catch it over the points of the skewer, tie it in the centre of the back, and be particular that the turkey is very firmly trussed. This may be more easily accomplished with a needle and twine than with skewers. *Mode.*—Fasten a sheet of buttered paper on to the breast of the bird, put it down to a bright fire, at some little distance *at first* (afterwards draw it nearer), and keep it well basted the whole of the time it is cooking. About ¼ hour before serving, remove the paper, dredge the turkey lightly with flour, and put a piece of butter into the basting-ladle; as the butter melts, baste the bird with it. When of a nice brown and well frothed, serve with a tureen of good brown gravy and one of bread sauce. Fried sausages are a favourite addition to roast turkey; they make a pretty garnish, besides adding very much to the flavour. When these are not at hand, a few forcemeat balls should be placed round the dish as a garnish. Turkey may also be stuffed with sausage-meat, and a chestnut forcemeat with the chestnut sauce is, by many persons, very much esteemed as an accompaniment to this favourite dish. *Time.*—Small turkey, 1½ hour; moderate-sized one, about 10 lbs., 2 hours; large turkey, 2½ hours, or longer. *Average cost*, from 10*s*. to 12*s*., but expensive at Christmas, on account of the great demand. *Sufficient.*—A moderate-sized turkey for 7 or 8 persons. *Seasonable* from December to February.

**ROAST TURKEY.**

## TURKEY, Roast.

A noble dish is a turkey, roast or boiled. A Christmas dinner, with the middle-classes of this empire, would scarcely be a Christmas dinner without its turkey; and we can hardly imagine an object of greater envy than is presented by a respected portly pater-familias carving, at the season devoted to good cheer and genial charity, his own fat turkey, and carving it well. The only art consists, as in the carving of a goose, in getting from the breast as many fine slices as possible; and all must have remarked the very great difference in the large number of people whom a good carver will find slices for, and the comparatively few that a bad carver will succeed in serving. As we have stated in both the carving of a duck and goose, the carver should commence cutting slices to the wing, from 2 to 3, and then proceed upwards towards the ridge of the breastbone: this is not the usual plan, but, in practice, will be found the best. The breast is the only part which is looked on as fine in a turkey, the legs being very seldom cut off and eaten at table: they are usually removed to the kitchen, where they are taken off, as here marked, to appear only in a form which seems to have a special attraction at a bachelor's supper-table,—we mean devilled: served in this way, they are especially liked and relished. A boiled turkey is carved in the same manner as when roasted.

**ROAST TURKEY.**

## TURKEY POULTS, Roast.

*Ingredients.*—Turkey poult; butter. *Choosing and Trussing.*—Choose a plump bird, and truss it in the following manner:—After it has been carefully plucked, drawn, and singed, skin the neck, and fasten the head under the wing; turn the legs at the first joint, and bring the feet close to the thighs, as a woodcock should be trussed, *and do not stuff it. Mode.*—Put it down to a bright fire, keep it well basted, and at first place a piece of paper on the breast to prevent its taking too much colour. About 10 minutes before serving, dredge it lightly with flour, and baste well; when nicely frothed, send it to table immediately, with a little gravy in the dish, and some in a tureen. If at hand, a few water-cresses may be placed round the turkey as a garnish, or it may be larded. *Time.*—About 1 hour. *Average cost*, 7*s.* to 8*s.* each. *Sufficient* for 6 or 7 persons. *Seasonable.*—In full season from June to October.

## TURKEY SOUP (a Seasonable Dish at Christmas).

*Ingredients.*—2 quarts of medium stock, the remains of a cold roast turkey, 2 oz. of rice-flour or arrowroot, salt and pepper to taste, 1 tablespoonful of Harvey's sauce or mushroom ketchup. *Mode.*—Cut up the turkey in small pieces, and put it in the stock; let it simmer slowly until the bones are quite clean. Take the bones out, and work the soup through a sieve; when cool, skim well. Mix the rice-flour or arrowroot to a batter with a little of the soup; add it with the seasoning and sauce, or ketchup. Give one boil, and serve. *Time.*—4 hours. *Average cost*, 10*d.* per quart. *Seasonable* at Christmas. *Sufficient* for 8 persons.

*Note.*—Instead of thickening this soup, vermicelli or macaroni may be served in it.

## TURNIP SOUP

*Ingredients.*—3 oz. of butter, 9 good-sized turnips, 4 onions, 2 quarts of stock, seasoning to taste. *Mode.*—Melt the butter in the stewpan, but do not let it boil; wash, drain, and slice the turnips and onions very thin; put them in the butter, with a teacupful of stock, and stew very gently for an hour. Then add the remainder of the stock, and simmer another hour. Rub it through a tammy, put it back into the stewpan, but do not let it boil. Serve very hot. *Time.*—2½ hours. *Average cost*, 8*d.* per quart. *Seasonable* from October to March. *Sufficient* for 8 persons.

*Note.*—By adding a little cream, this soup will be much improved.

## TURNIPS, Boiled.

*Ingredients.*—Turnips; to each ½ gallon of water allow 1 heaped tablespoonful of salt. *Mode.*—Pare the turnips, and, should they be very large, divide them into quarters; but, unless this is the case, let them be cooked whole. Put them into a saucepan of boiling water, salted in the above proportion, and let them boil gently until tender. Try them with a fork, and, when done, take them up in a colander; let them thoroughly drain, and serve. Boiled turnips are usually sent to table with boiled mutton, but are infinitely nicer when mashed than served whole: unless nice and young, they are scarcely worth the trouble of dressing plainly as above. *Time.*—Old turnips, ¾ to 1¼ hour; young ones, about 18 to 20 minutes. *Average cost*, 4*d.* per bunch. *Sufficient.*—Allow a bunch of 12 turnips for 5 or 6 persons. *Seasonable.*—May be had all the year; but in spring only useful for flavouring gravies, &c.

TURNIPS, German Mode of Cooking.

*Ingredients.*—8 large turnips, 3 oz. of butter, pepper and salt to taste, rather more than ½ pint of weak stock or broth, 1 tablespoonful of flour. *Mode.*—Make the butter hot in a stewpan, lay in the turnips, after having pared and cut them into dice, and season them with pepper and salt. Toss them over the fire for a few minutes, then add the broth, and simmer the whole gently till the turnips are tender. Brown the above proportion of flour with a little butter; add this to the turnips, let them simmer another 5 minutes, and serve. Boiled mutton is usually sent to table with this vegetable, and may be cooked with the turnips by placing it in the midst of them: the meat would then be very delicious, as, there being so little liquid with the turnips, it would almost be steamed, and, consequently, very tender. *Time.*—20 minutes. *Average cost,* 4*d.* per bunch. *Sufficient* for 4 persons. *Seasonable.*—May be had all the year.

## TURNIPS, Mashed.

*Ingredients.*—10 or 12 large turnips; to each ½ gallon of water allow 1 heaped tablespoonful of salt, 2 oz. of butter, cayenne or white paper to taste. *Mode.*—Pare the turnips, quarter them, and put them into boiling water, salted in the above proportion; boil them until tender; then drain them in a colander, and squeeze them as dry as possible by pressing them with the back of a large plate. When quite free from water, rub the turnips with a wooden spoon through the colander, and put them into a very clean saucepan; add the butter, white pepper, or cayenne, and, if necessary, a little salt. Keep stirring them over the fire until the butter is well mixed with them, and the turnips are thoroughly hot; dish, and serve. A little cream or milk added after the turnips are pressed through the colander, is an improvement to both the colour and flavour of this vegetable. *Time.*—From ½ to ¾ hour to boil the turnips; 10 minutes to warm them through. *Average cost,* 4*d.* per bunch. *Sufficient* for 4 or 5 persons. *Seasonable.*—May be had all the year; but in early spring only good for flavouring gravies.

## TURNIPS IN WHITE SAUCE. (An Entremets, or to be served with the Second Course as a Side-dish.)

*Ingredients.*—7 or 8 turnips, 1 oz. of butter, ½ pint of white sauce. *Mode.*—Peel and cut the turnips in the shape of pears or marbles; boil them in salt and water, to which has been added a little butter, until tender; then take them out, drain, arrange them on a dish, and pour over the white sauce made by either of the recipes, and to which has been added a small lump of sugar. In winter, when other vegetables are scarce, this will be found a very good and pretty-looking dish: when approved, a little mustard may be added to the sauce. *Time.*—About ¾ hour to boil the turnips. *Average cost,* 4d. per bunch. *Sufficient* for 1 side dish. *Seasonable* in winter.

## VANILLA CUSTARD SAUCE, to serve with Puddings.

*Ingredients.*—½ pint of milk, 2 eggs, 2 oz. of sugar, 10 drops of essence of vanilla. *Mode.*—Beat the eggs, sweeten the milk; stir these ingredients well together, and flavour them with essence of vanilla, regulating the proportion of this latter ingredient by the strength of the essence, the size of the eggs, &c. Put the mixture into a small jug, place this jug in a saucepan of boiling water, and stir the sauce *one way* until it thickens; but do not allow it to boil, or it will instantly curdle. Serve in a boat or tureen separately, with plum, bread, or any kind of dry pudding. Essence of bitter almonds or lemon-rind may be substituted for the vanilla, when they are more in accordance with the flavouring of the pudding with which the sauce is intended to be served. *Time.*—To be stirred in the jug from 8 to 10 minutes. *Average cost,* 4d. *Sufficient* for 4 or 5 persons.

## VEAL, Baked (Cold Meat Cookery).

*Ingredients.*—½ lb. of cold roast veal, a few slices of bacon, 1 pint of bread-crumbs, ½ pint of good veal gravy, ½ teaspoonful of minced lemon-peel, 1 blade of pounded mace, cayenne and salt to taste, 4 eggs. *Mode.*—Mince finely the veal and bacon; add the bread-crumbs, gravy, and seasoning, and stir these ingredients well together. Beat up the eggs thoroughly; add these, mix the whole well together, put into a dish, and bake from ¾ to 1 hour. When liked, a little good gravy may be served in a tureen as an accompaniment. *Time.*—from ¾ to 1 hour. *Average cost,* exclusive of the cold meat, 6d. *Sufficient* for 3 or 4 persons. *Seasonable* from March to October.

## VEAL, Roast Breast of.

*Ingredients.*—Veal; a little flour. *Mode.*—Wash the veal, well wipe it, and dredge it with flour; put it down to a bright fire, not too near, as it should not be scorched. Baste it plentifully until done; dish it, pour over the meat some good melted butter, and send to table with it a piece of boiled bacon and a cut lemon. *Time.*—From 1½ to 2 hours. *Average cost,* 8½d. per lb. *Sufficient* for 5 or 6 persons. *Seasonable* from March to October.

## VEAL, Breast of, to Carve.

The carving of a breast of veal is not dissimilar to that of a fore-quarter of lamb, when the shoulder has been taken off. The breast of veal consists of two parts,—the rib-bones and the gristly brisket. These two parts should first be separated by sharply passing the knife in the direction of the lines 1, 2; when they are entirely divided, the rib-bones should be carved in the direction of the lines 5 to 6; and the brisket can be helped by cutting pieces in the direction 3 to 4. The carver should ask the guests whether they have a preference for the brisket or ribs; and if there be a sweetbread served with the dish, as it often is with roast breast of veal, each person should receive a piece.

**BREAST OF VEAL.**

## VEAL, Stewed Breast of, and Peas.

*Ingredients.*—Breast of veal, 2 oz. of butter, a bunch of savoury herbs, including parsley; 2 blades of pounded mace, 2 cloves, 5 or 6 young onions, 1 strip of lemon-peel, 6 allspice, ¼ teaspoonful of pepper, 1 teaspoonful of salt, thickening of butter and flour, 2 tablespoonfuls of sherry, 2 tablespoonfuls of tomato sauce, 1 tablespoonful of lemon-juice, 2 tablespoonfuls of mushroom ketchup, green peas. *Mode.*—Cut the breast in half, after removing the bone underneath, and divide the meat into convenient-sized pieces. Put the butter into a frying-pan, lay in the pieces of veal, and fry until of a nice brown colour. Now place these in a stewpan with the herbs, mace, cloves, onions, lemon-peel, allspice, and seasoning; pour over them just sufficient boiling water to cover the meat; well close the lid, and let the whole simmer very gently for about 2 hours. Strain off as much gravy as is required, thicken it with butter and flour, add the remaining ingredients, skim well, let it simmer for about 10 minutes, then pour it over the meat. Have ready some green peas, boiled separately; sprinkle these over the veal, and serve. It may be garnished with forcemeat balls, or rashers of bacon curled and fried. Instead of cutting up the meat, many persons prefer it dressed whole;—in that case it should be half-roasted before the water, &c. are put to it. *Time.*—2¼ hours. *Average cost,* 8½*d. Sufficient* for 5 or 6 persons. *Seasonable* from March to October.

## VEAL, à la Bourgeoise (Excellent).

*Ingredients.*—2 to 3 lbs. of the loin or neck of veal, 10 or 12 young carrots, a bunch of green onions, 2 slices of lean bacon, 2 blades of pounded mace, 1 bunch of savoury herbs, pepper and salt to taste, a few new potatoes, 1 pint of green peas. *Mode.*—Cut the veal into cutlets, trim them, and put the trimmings into a stewpan with a little butter; lay in the cutlets and fry them a nice brown colour on both sides. Add the bacon, carrots, onions, spice, herbs, and seasoning; pour in about a pint of boiling water, and stew gently for 2 hours on a very slow fire. When done, skim off the fat, take out the herbs, and flavour the gravy with a little tomato sauce and ketchup. Have ready the peas and potatoes, boiled *separately*; put them with the veal, and serve. *Time.*—2 hours. *Average cost,* 2*s.* 9*d. Sufficient* for 5 or 6 persons. *Seasonable* from June to August with peas;—rather earlier when these are omitted.

## VEAL CAKE (a Convenient Dish for a Picnic).

*Ingredients.*—A few slices of cold roast veal, a few slices of cold ham, 2 hard-boiled eggs, 2 tablespoonfuls of minced parsley, a little pepper, good gravy. *Mode.*—Cut off all the brown outside from the veal, and cut the eggs into slices. Procure a pretty mould; lay veal, ham, eggs, and parsley in layers, with a little pepper between each, and when the mould is full, get some *strong* stock, and fill up the shape. Bake for ½ hour, and when cold, turn it out. *Time.*—½ hour. *Seasonable* at any time.

## VEAL, Curried (Cold Meat Cookery).

*Ingredients.*—The remains of cold roast veal, 4 onions, 2 apples sliced, 1 tablespoonful of curry-powder, 1 dessertspoonful of flour, ½ pint of broth or water, 1 tablespoonful of lemon-juice. *Mode.*—Slice the onions and apples, and fry them in a little butter; then take them out, cut the meat into neat cutlets, and fry these of a pale brown; add the curry-powder and flour, put in the onion, apples, and a little broth or water, and stew gently till quite tender; add the lemon-juice, and serve with an edging of boiled rice. The curry may be ornamented with pickles, capsicums, and gherkins, arranged prettily on the top. *Time.*—¾ hour. *Average cost*, exclusive of the meat, 4*d*. *Seasonable* from March to October.

## VEAL CUTLETS (an Entrée).

*Ingredients.*—About 3 lbs. of the prime part of the leg of veal, egg and bread-crumbs, 3 tablespoonfuls of minced savoury herbs, salt and pepper to taste, a small piece of butter. *Mode.*—Have the veal cut into slices about ¾ of an inch in thickness, and, if not cut perfectly even, level the meat with a cutlet-bat or rolling-pin. Shape and trim the cutlets, and brush them over with egg. Sprinkle with bread-crumbs, with which have been mixed minced herbs and a seasoning of pepper and salt, and press the crumbs down. Fry them of a delicate brown in fresh lard or butter, and be careful not to burn them. They should be very thoroughly done, but not dry. If the cutlets be thick, keep the pan covered for a few minutes at a good distance from the fire, after they have acquired a good colour: by this means, the meat will be done through. Lay the cutlets in a dish, keep them hot, and make a gravy in the pan as follows:—Dredge in a little flour, add a piece of butter the size of a walnut, brown it, then pour as much boiling water as is required over it, season with pepper and salt, add a little lemon-juice, give one boil, and pour it over the cutlets. They should be garnished with slices of broiled bacon, and a few forcemeat balls will be found a very excellent addition to this dish. *Time.*—For cutlets of a moderate thickness, about 12 minutes; if very thick, allow more time. *Average cost*, 10*d.* per lb. *Sufficient* for 6 persons. *Seasonable* from March to October.

VEAL CUTLETS.

*Note.*—Veal cutlets may be merely floured and fried of a nice brown: the gravy and garnishing should be the same as in the preceding recipe. They may also be cut from the loin or neck, as shown in the engraving.

### VEAL CUTLETS, Broiled, à la Italienne (an Entrée).

*Ingredients.*—Neck of veal, salt and pepper to taste, the yolk of 1 egg, bread-crumbs, ½ pint of Italian sauce. *Mode.*—Cut the veal into cutlets, flatten and trim them nicely; powder over them a little salt and pepper; brush them over with the yolk of an egg, dip them into bread-crumbs, then into clarified butter, and, afterwards, in the bread-crumbs again; boil or fry them over a clear fire, that they may acquire a good brown colour. Arrange them in the dish alternately with rashers of broiled ham, and pour the sauce (made by recipe for Italian sauce, p. 305) in the middle. *Time.*—10 to 15 minutes, according to the thickness of the cutlets. *Average cost*, 10*d.* per lb. *Seasonable* from March to October.

### VEAL CUTLETS, à la Maintenon (an Entrée).

*Ingredients.*—2 or 3 lbs. of veal cutlets, egg and bread-crumbs, 2 tablespoonfuls of minced savoury herbs, salt and pepper to taste, a little grated nutmeg. *Mode.*—Cut the cutlets about ¾ inch in thickness, flatten them, and brush them over with the yolk of an egg; dip them into bread-crumbs and minced herbs, season with pepper and salt and grated nutmeg, and fold each cutlet in a piece of buttered paper. Broil them, and send them to table with melted butter or a good gravy. *Time.*—From 15 to 18 minutes. *Average cost*, 10*d.* per lb. *Sufficient* for 5 or 6 persons. *Seasonable* from March to October.

### VEAL, Fillet of, au Béchamel (Cold Meat Cookery).

*Ingredients.*—A small fillet of veal, 1 pint of béchamel sauce, a few bread-crumbs, clarified butter. *Mode.*—A fillet of veal that has been roasted the preceding day will answer very well for this dish. Cut the middle out rather deep, leaving a good margin round, from which to cut nice slices, and if there should be any cracks in the veal, fill them up with forcemeat. Mince finely the meat that was taken out, mixing with it a little of the forcemeat to flavour, and stir to it sufficient béchamel to make it of a proper consistency. Warm the veal in the oven for about an hour, taking care to baste it well, that it may not be dry; put the mince in the place where the meat was taken out, sprinkle a few bread-crumbs over it, and drop a little clarified butter on the bread-crumbs; put it into the oven for ¼ hour to brown, and pour béchamel round the sides of the dish. *Time.*—Altogether 1½ hour. *Seasonable* from March to October.

## VEAL, Roast Fillet of.

*Ingredients.*—Veal, forcemeat, melted butter. *Mode.*—Have the fillet cut according to the size required; take out the bone, and after raising the skin from the meat, put under the flap a nice forcemeat. Prepare sufficient of this, as there should be some left to eat cold, and to season and flavour a mince if required. Skewer and bind the veal up in a round form; dredge well with flour, put it down at some distance from the fire at first, and baste continually. About ½ hour before serving, draw it nearer the fire, that it may acquire more colour, as the outside should be of a rich brown, but not burnt. Dish it, remove the skewers, which replace by a silver one; pour over the joint some good melted butter, and serve with either boiled ham, bacon, or pickled pork. Never omit to send a cut lemon to table with roast veal. *Time.*—A fillet of veal weighing 12 lbs., about 4 hours. *Average cost*, 9d. per lb. *Sufficient* for 9 or 10 persons. *Seasonable* from March to October.

**FILLET OF VEAL.**

## VEAL, Fillet of.

The carving of this joint is similar to that of a round of beef. Slices, not too thick, in the direction of the line 1 to 2 are cut; and the only point to be careful about is, that the veal be *evenly* carved. Between the flap and the meat the stuffing is inserted, and a small portion of this should be served to every guest. The persons whom the host wishes most to honour should be asked if they like the delicious brown outside slice, as this, by many, is exceedingly relished.

**FILLET OF VEAL.**

## VEAL, Stewed Fillet of.

*Ingredients.*—A small fillet of veal, forcemeat, thickening of butter and flour, a few mushrooms, white pepper to taste, 2 tablespoonfuls of lemon-juice, 2 blades of pounded mace, ½ glass of sherry. *Mode.*—If the whole of the leg is purchased, take off the knuckle to stew, and also the square end, which will serve for cutlets or pies. Remove the bone, and fill the space with a forcemeat. Roll and skewer it up firmly; place a few skewers at the bottom of a stewpan to prevent the meat from sticking, and cover the veal with a little weak stock. Let it simmer very *gently* until tender, as the more slowly veal is stewed, the better. Strain and thicken the sauce, flavour it with lemon-juice, mace, sherry, and white pepper; give one boil, and pour it over the meat. The skewers should be removed, and replaced by a silver one, and the dish garnished with slices of cut lemon. *Time.*—A fillet of veal weighing 6 lbs., 3 hours' very gentle stewing. *Average cost*, 9*d.* per lb. *Sufficient* for 5 or 6 persons. *Seasonable* from March to October.

## VEAL, Fricandeau of (an Entrée).

**FRICANDEAU OF VEAL.**

*Ingredients.*—A piece of the fat side of a leg of veal (about 3 lbs.), lardoons, 2 carrots, 2 large onions, a faggot of savoury herbs, 2 blades of pounded mace, 6 whole allspice, 2 bay-leaves, pepper to taste, a few slices of fat bacon, 1 pint of stock. *Mode.*—The veal for a fricandeau should be of the best quality, or it will not be good. It may be known by the meat being white and not thready. Take off the skin, flatten the veal on the table, then at one stroke of the knife, cut off as much as is required, for a fricandeau with an uneven surface never looks well. Trim it, and with a sharp knife make two or three slits in the middle, that it may taste more of the seasoning. Now lard it thickly with fat bacon, as lean gives a red colour to the fricandeau. Slice the vegetables, and put these, with the herbs and spices, in the *middle* of a stewpan, with a few slices of bacon at the top: these should form a sort of mound in the centre for the veal to rest upon. Lay the fricandeau over the bacon, sprinkle over it a little salt, and pour in just sufficient stock to cover the bacon, &c., without touching the veal. Let it gradually come to a boil; then put it over a slow and equal fire, and let it *simmer very* gently for about 2½ hours, or longer should it be very large. Baste it frequently with the liquor, and a short time before serving, put it into a brisk oven, to make the bacon firm, which otherwise would break when it was glazed. Dish the fricandeau, keep it hot, skim off the fat from the liquor, and reduce it quickly to a glaze, with which glaze the fricandeau, and serve with a purée of whatever vegetable happens to be in season—spinach, sorrel, asparagus, cucumbers, peas, &c. *Time.*—2½ hours. If very large, allow more time. *Average cost*, 3*s.* 6*d. Sufficient* for an entrée. *Seasonable* from March to October.

## VEAL, Fricandeau of (more economical).

*Ingredients.*—The best end of a neck of veal (about 2½ lbs.), lardoons, 2 carrots, 2 onions, a faggot of savoury herbs, 2 blades of mace, 2 bay-leaves, a little whole white pepper, a few slices of fat bacon. *Mode.*—Cut away the lean part of the best end of a neck of veal with a sharp knife, scooping it from the bones. Put the bones in with a little water, which will serve to moisten the fricandeau; they should stew about 1½ hour. Lard the veal, proceed in the same way as in the preceding recipe, and be careful that the gravy does not touch the fricandeau. Stew very gently for 3 hours; glaze, and serve it on sorrel, spinach, or with a little gravy in the dish. *Time.*—3 hours. *Average cost*, 2s. 6d. *Sufficient* for an entrée. *Seasonable* from March to October.

*Note.*—When the prime part of the leg is cut off, it spoils the whole; consequently, to use this for a fricandeau is rather extravagant. The best end of the neck answers the purpose nearly or quite as well.

## VEAL, to Carve a Knuckle of.

The engraving, showing the dotted line from 1 to 2, sufficiently indicates the direction which should be given to the knife in carving this dish. The best slices are those from the thickest part of the knuckle, that is, outside the line 1 to 2.

**KNUCKLE OF VEAL.**

## VEAL, to Ragoût a Knuckle of.

*Ingredients.*—Knuckle of veal, pepper and salt to taste, flour, 1 onion, 1 head of celery, or a little celery-seed, a faggot of savoury herbs, 2 blades of pounded mace, thickening of butter and flour, a few young carrots, 1 tablespoonful of tomato sauce, 3 tablespoonfuls of sherry, the juice of ½ lemon. *Mode.*—Cut the meat from a knuckle of veal into neat slices, season with pepper and salt, and dredge them with flour. Fry them in a little butter of a pale brown, and put them into a stewpan with the bone (which should be chopped in several places); add the celery, herbs, mace, and carrots; pour over all about 1 pint of hot water, and let it simmer very gently for 2 hours over a slow but clear fire. Take out the slices of meat and carrots, strain and thicken the gravy with a little butter rolled in flour; add the remaining ingredients, give one boil, put back the meat and carrots, let these get hot through, and serve. When in season, a few green peas, *boiled separately*, and added to this dish at the moment of serving, would be found a very agreeable addition. *Time.*—2 hours. *Average cost,* 5*d.* to 6*d.* per lb. *Sufficient* for 4 or 5 persons.

## VEAL, Stewed Knuckle of, and Rice.

*Ingredients.*—Knuckle of veal, 1 onion, 2 blades of mace, 1 teaspoonful of salt, ½ lb. of rice. *Mode.*—Have the knuckle cut small, or cut some cutlets from it, that it may be just large enough to be eaten the same day it is dressed, as cold boiled veal is not a particularly tempting dish. Break the shank-bone, wash it clean, and put the meat into a stewpan with sufficient water to cover it. Let it gradually come to a boil, put in the salt, and remove the scum as fast as it rises. When it has simmered gently for about ¾ hour, add the remaining ingredients, and stew the whole gently for 2¼ hours. Put the meat into a deep dish, pour over it the rice, &c., and send boiled bacon, and a tureen of parsley and butter to table with it. *Time.*—A knuckle of veal weighing 6 lbs., 3 hours' gentle stewing. *Average cost,* 5*d.* to 6*d.* per lb. *Sufficient* for 5 or 6 persons. *Seasonable* from March to October.

**KNUCKLE OF VEAL.**

*Note.*—Macaroni, instead of rice, boiled with the veal, will be found good; or the rice and macaroni may be omitted, and the veal sent to table smothered in parsley and butter.

## VEAL, Roast Loin of.

*Ingredients.*—Veal; melted butter. *Mode.*—Paper the kidney fat; roll in and skewer the flap, which makes the joint a good shape; dredge it well with flour, and put it down to a bright fire. Should the loin be very large, skewer the kidney back for a time to roast thoroughly. Keep it well basted, and a short time before serving, remove the paper from the kidney, and allow it to acquire a nice brown colour, but it should not be burnt. Have ready some melted butter, put it into the dripping-pan after it is emptied of its contents, pour it over the veal, and serve. Garnish the dish with slices of lemon and forcemeat balls, and send to table with it boiled bacon, ham, pickled pork, or pig's cheek. *Time.*—A large loin, 3 hours. *Average cost*, 9½d. per lb. *Sufficient* for 7 or 8 persons. *Seasonable* from March to October.

**LOIN OF VEAL.**

*Note.*—A piece of toast should be placed under the kidneys when the veal is dished.

## VEAL, Loin of, au Béchamel (Cold Meat Cookery).

*Ingredients.*—Loin of veal, ½ teaspoonful of minced lemon-peel, rather more than ½ pint of béchamel or white sauce, *Mode.*—A loin of veal which has come from table with very little taken off, answers well for this dish. Cut off the meat from the inside, mince it, and mix with it some minced lemon-peel; put it into sufficient béchamel to warm it through. In the mean time, wrap the joint in buttered paper, and place it in the oven to warm. When thoroughly hot, dish the mince, place the loin above it, and pour over the remainder of the béchamel. *Time.*—1½ hour to warm the meat in the oven. *Seasonable* from March to October.

## VEAL, Loin of, à la Daube.

*Ingredients.*—The chump end of a loin of veal, forcemeat, a few slices of bacon, a bunch of savoury herbs, 2 blades of mace, ½ teaspoonful of whole white pepper, 1 pint of veal stock or water, 5 or 6 green onions. *Mode.*—Cut off the chump from a loin of veal, and take out the bone; fill the cavity with forcemeat, tie it up tightly, and lay it in a stewpan with the bones and trimmings, and cover the veal with a few slices of bacon. Add the herbs, mace, pepper, and onions, and stock or water; cover the pan with a closely-fitting lid, and simmer for 2 hours, shaking the stewpan occasionally. Take out the bacon, herbs, and onions; reduce the gravy, if not already thick enough, to a glaze, with which glaze the meat, and serve with tomato, mushroom, or sorrel sauce. *Time.*—2 hours. *Average cost*, 9*d*. per lb. *Sufficient* for 4 or 5 persons. *Seasonable* from March to October.

## VEAL, to Carve Loin of.

As is the case with a loin of mutton, the careful jointing of a loin of veal is more than half the battle in carving it. If the butcher be negligent in this matter, he should be admonished; for there is nothing more annoying or irritating to an inexperienced carver than to be obliged to turn his knife in all directions to find the exact place where it should be inserted in order to divide the bones. When the jointing is properly performed, there is little difficulty in carrying the knife down in the direction of the line 1 to 2. To each guest should be given a piece of the kidney and kidney fat, which lie underneath, and are considered great delicacies.

**LOIN OF VEAL.**

## VEAL, Minced, with Béchamel Sauce (Cold Meat Cookery, very good).

*Ingredients.*—The remains of a fillet of veal, 1 pint of béchamel sauce, ½ teaspoonful of minced lemon-peel, forcemeat balls. *Mode.*—Cut—but do not *chop*—a few slices of cold roast veal as finely as possible, sufficient to make rather more than 1 lb., weighed after being minced. Make the above proportion of béchamel, by recipe; add the lemon-peel, put in the veal, and let the whole gradually warm through. When it is at the point of simmering, dish it, and garnish with forcemeat balls and fried sippets of bread. *Time.*— To simmer 1 minute. *Average cost,* exclusive of the cold meat, 1*s.* 4*d.* *Sufficient* for 5 or 6 persons. *Seasonable* from March to October.

## VEAL, Minced (more economical).

*Ingredients.*—The remains of cold roast fillet or loin of veal, rather more than 1 pint of water, 1 onion, ½ teaspoonful of minced lemon-peel, salt and white pepper to taste, 1 blade of pounded mace, 2 or 3 young carrots, a faggot of sweet herbs, thickening of butter and flour, a tablespoonful of lemon-juice, 3 tablespoonfuls of cream or milk. *Mode.*—Take about 1 lb. of veal, and should there be any bones, dredge them with flour, and put them into a stewpan with the brown outside, and a few meat trimmings, add rather more than a pint of water, the onion cut in slices, lemon-peel, seasoning, mace, carrots, and herbs; simmer these well for rather more than 1 hour, and strain the liquor. Rub a little flour into some butter; add this to the gravy, set it on the fire, and, when it boils, skim well. Mince the veal finely by *cutting*, and not chopping it; put it in the gravy; let it get warmed through gradually; add the lemon-juice and cream, and, when it is on the point of boiling, serve. Garnish the dish with sippets of toasted bread and slices of bacon rolled and toasted. Forcemeat balls may also be added. If more lemon-peel is liked than is stated above, put a little very finely minced to the veal, after it is warmed in the gravy. *Time.*—1 hour to make the gravy. *Average cost,* exclusive of the cold meat, 6*d. Seasonable* from March to October.

## VEAL, Minced, and Macaroni (a pretty side or corner dish).

*Ingredients.*—¾ lb. of minced cold roast veal, 3 oz. of ham, 1 tablespoonful of gravy, pepper and salt to taste, ¼ teaspoonful of grated nutmeg, ¼ lb. of bread-crumbs, ¼ lb. of macaroni, 1 or 2 eggs to bind, a small piece of butter. *Mode.*—Cut some nice slices from a cold fillet of veal, trim off the brown outside, and mince the meat finely with the above proportion of ham: should the meat be very dry, add a spoonful of good gravy. Season highly with pepper and salt, add the grated nutmeg and bread-crumbs, and mix these ingredients with 1 or 2 eggs well beaten, which should bind the mixture and make it like forcemeat. In the mean time, boil the macaroni in salt and water, and drain it; butter a mould, put some of the macaroni at the bottom and sides of it, in whatever form is liked; mix the remainder with the forcemeat, fill the mould up to the top, put a plate or small dish on it, and steam for ½ hour. Turn it out carefully, and serve with good gravy poured round, but not over, the meat. *Time.*—½ hour. *Average cost,* exclusive of the cold meat, 10*d. Seasonable* from March to October.

*Note.*—To make a variety, boil some carrots and turnips separately in a little salt and water; when done, cut them into pieces about ⅛ inch in thickness; butter an oval mould, and place these in it, in white and red stripes alternately, at the bottom and sides. Proceed as in the foregoing recipe, and be very careful in turning it out of the mould.

## VEAL, Moulded Minced (Cold Meat Cookery).

*Ingredients.*—¾ lb. of cold roast veal, a small slice of bacon, 1/3 teaspoonful of minced lemon-peel, ½ onion chopped fine, salt, pepper, and pounded mace to taste, a slice of toast soaked in milk, 1 egg. *Mode.*—Mince the meat very fine, after removing from it all skin and outside pieces, and chop the bacon; mix these well together, adding the lemon-peel, onion, seasoning, mace, and toast. When all the ingredients are thoroughly incorporated, beat up an egg, with which bind the mixture. Butter a shape, put in the meat, and bake for ¾ hour; turn it out of the mould carefully, and pour round it a good brown gravy. A sheep's head dressed in this manner is an economical and savoury dish. *Time.*—¾ hour. *Average* cost, exclusive of the meat, 6*d. Seasonable* from March to October.

## VEAL, Braised Neck of.

*Ingredients.*—The best end of the neck of veal (from 3 to 4 lbs.), bacon, 1 tablespoonful of minced parsley, salt, pepper, and grated nutmeg to taste; 1 onion, 2 carrots, a little celery (when this is not obtainable, use the seed), ½ glass of sherry, thickening of butter and flour, lemon-juice, 1 blade of pounded mace. *Mode.*—Prepare the bacon for larding, and roll it in minced parsley, salt, pepper, and grated nutmeg; lard the veal, put it into a stewpan with a few slices of lean bacon or ham, an onion, carrots, and celery; and do not quite cover it with water. Stew it gently for 2 hours, or until it is quite tender; strain off the liquor; stir together over the fire, in a stewpan, a little flour and butter until brown; lay the veal in this, the upper side to the bottom of the pan, and let it remain till it is a nice brown colour. Place it in the dish; pour into the stewpan as much gravy as is required, boil it up, skim well, add the wine, pounded mace, and lemon-juice; simmer for 3 minutes, pour it over the meat, and serve. *Time.*—Rather more than 2 hours. *Average cost*, 8*d.* per lb. *Sufficient* for 5 or 6 persons. *Seasonable* from March to October.

## VEAL, Roast Neck of.

*Ingredients.*—Veal, melted butter, forcemeat balls. *Mode.*—Have the veal cut from the best end of the neck; dredge it with flour, and put it down to a bright clear fire; keep it well basted; dish it, pour over it some melted butter, and garnish the dish with fried forcemeat balls; send to table with a cut lemon. The scrag may be boiled or stewed in various ways, with rice, onion-sauce, or parsley and butter. *Time.*—About 2 hours. *Average cost*, 8*d.* per lb. *Sufficient.*—4 or 5 lbs. for 5 or 6 persons. *Seasonable* from March to October.

## VEAL OLIVE PIE (Cold Meat Cookery).

*Ingredients.*—A few thin slices of cold fillet of veal, a few thin slices of bacon, forcemeat, a cupful of gravy, 4 tablespoonfuls of cream, puff-crust. *Mode.*—Cut thin slices from a fillet of veal, place on them thin slices of bacon, and over them a layer of forcemeat, made by recipe, with an additional seasoning of shalot and cayenne; roll them tightly, and fill up a pie-dish with them; add the gravy and cream, cover with a puff-crust, and bake for 1 to 1½ hour: should the pie be very large, allow 2 hours. The pieces of rolled veal should be about 3 inches in length, and about 3 inches round. *Time.*—Moderate-sized pie, 1 to 1½ hour. *Seasonable* from March to October.

## VEAL PIE.

*Ingredients.*—2 lbs. of veal cutlets, 1 or 2 slices of lean bacon or ham, pepper and salt to taste, 2 tablespoonfuls of minced savoury herbs, 2 blades of pounded mace, crust, 1 teacupful of gravy. *Mode.*—Cut the cutlets into square pieces, and season them with pepper, salt, and pounded mace; put them in a pie-dish with the savoury herbs sprinkled over, and 1 or 2 slices of lean bacon or ham placed at the top: if possible, this should be previously cooked, as undressed bacon makes the veal red, and spoils its appearance. Pour in a little water, cover with crust, ornament it in any way that is approved; brush it over with the yolk of an egg, and bake in a well-heated oven for about 1½ hour. Pour in a good gravy after baking, which is done by removing the top ornament, and replacing it after the gravy is added. *Time.*—About 1½ hour. *Average cost*, 2*s.* 6*d. Sufficient* for 5 or 6 persons. *Seasonable* from March to October.

## VEAL AND HAM PIE.

*Ingredients.*—2 lbs. of veal cutlets, ½ lb. of boiled ham, 2 tablespoonfuls of minced savoury herbs, ¼ teaspoonful of grated nutmeg, 2 blades of pounded mace, pepper and salt to taste, a strip of lemon-peel finely minced, the yolks of 2 hard-boiled eggs, ½ pint of water, nearly ½ pint of good strong gravy, puff-crust. *Mode.*—Cut the veal into nice square pieces, and put a layer of them at the bottom of a pie-dish; sprinkle over these a portion of the herbs, spices, seasoning, lemon-peel, and the yolks of the eggs cut in slices; cut the ham very thin, and put a layer of this in. Proceed in this manner until the dish is full, so arranging it that the ham comes at the top. Lay a puff paste on the edge of the dish, and pour in about ½ pint of water; cover with crust, ornament it with leaves, brush it over with the yolk of an egg, and bake in a well-heated oven for 1 to 1½ hour, or longer, should the pie be very large. When it is taken out of the oven, pour in at the top, through a funnel, nearly ½ pint of strong gravy: this should be made sufficiently good that, when cold, it may cut in a firm jelly. This pie may be very much enriched by adding a few mushrooms, oysters, or sweetbreads; but it will be found very good without any of the last-named additions. *Time.*—1½ hour, or longer, should the pie be very large. *Average cost*, 3*s. Sufficient* for 5 or 6 persons. *Seasonable* from March to October.

## VEAL, Potted (for Breakfast).

*Ingredients.*—To every lb. of veal allow ¼ lb. of ham, cayenne and pounded mace to taste, 6 oz. of fresh butter; clarified butter. *Mode.*—Mince the veal and ham together as finely as possible, and pound well in a mortar, with cayenne, pounded mace, and fresh butter in the above proportion. When reduced to a perfectly smooth paste, press it into potting-pots, and cover with clarified butter. If kept in a cool place, it will remain good some days. *Seasonable* from March to October.

## VEAL, Ragoût of Cold (Cold Meat Cookery).

*Ingredients.*—The remains of cold veal, 1 oz. of butter, ½ pint of gravy, thickening of butter and flour, pepper and salt to taste, 1 blade of pounded mace, 1 tablespoonful of mushroom ketchup, 1 tablespoonful of sherry, 1 dessertspoonful of lemon-juice, forcemeat balls. *Mode.*—Any part of veal will make this dish. Cut the meat into nice-looking pieces, put them in a stewpan with 1 oz. of butter, and fry a light brown; add the gravy (hot water may be substituted for this), thicken with a little butter and flour, and stew gently about ¼ hour; season with pepper, salt, and pounded mace; add the ketchup, sherry, and lemon-juice; give one boil, and serve. Garnish the dish with forcemeat balls and fried rashers of bacon. *Time.*—Altogether ½ hour. *Average cost,* exclusive of cold meat, 6d. *Seasonable* from March to October.

*Note.*—The above recipe may be varied, by adding vegetables, such as peas, cucumbers, lettuces, green onions cut in slices, a dozen or two of green gooseberries (not seedy), all of which should be fried a little with the meat, and then stewed in the gravy.

## VEAL RISSOLES (Cold Meat Cookery).

*Ingredients.*—A few slices of cold roast veal, a few slices of ham or bacon, 1 tablespoonful of minced parsley, 1 tablespoonful of minced savoury herbs, 1 blade of pounded mace, a very little grated nutmeg, cayenne and salt to taste, 2 eggs well beaten, bread-crumbs. *Mode.*—Mince the veal very finely with a little ham or bacon; add the parsley, herbs, spices, and seasoning; mix into a paste with an egg; form into balls or cones; brush these over with egg, sprinkle with bread-crumbs, and fry a rich brown. Serve with brown gravy, and garnish the dish with fried parsley.

*Time.*—About 10 minutes to fry the rissoles. *Seasonable* from March to October.

## VEAL ROLLS (Cold Meat Cookery).

*Ingredients.*—The remains of a cold fillet of veal, egg and bread-crumbs, a few slices of fat bacon, forcemeat. *Mode.*—Cut a few slices from a cold fillet of veal ½ inch thick; rub them over with egg; lay a thin slice of fat bacon over each piece of veal; brush these with the egg, and over this spread the forcemeat thinly; roll up each piece tightly, egg and bread-crumb them, and fry them a rich brown. Serve with mushroom sauce or brown gravy. *Time.*—10 to 15 minutes to fry the rolls. *Seasonable* from March to October.

## VEAL, Stuffed and Stewed Shoulder of.

*Ingredients.*—A shoulder of veal, a few slices of ham or bacon, forcemeat, 3 carrots, 2 onions, salt and pepper to taste, a faggot of savoury herbs, 3 blades of pounded mace, water, thickening of butter and flour. *Mode.*—Bone the joint by carefully detaching the meat from the blade-bone on one side, and then on the other, being particular not to pierce the skin; then cut the bone from the knuckle, and take it out. Fill the cavity whence the bone was taken with a forcemeat. Roll and bind the veal up tightly; put it into a stewpan with the carrots, onions, seasoning, herbs, and mace; pour in just sufficient water to cover it, and let it stew *very gently* for about 5 hours. Before taking it up, try if it is properly done by thrusting a larding-needle in it: if it penetrates easily, it is sufficiently cooked. Strain and skim the gravy, thicken with butter and flour, give one boil, and pour it round the meat. A few young carrots may be boiled and placed round the dish as a garnish, and, when in season, green peas should always be served with this dish. *Time.*—5 hours. *Average cost*, 7d. per lb. *Sufficient* for 8 or 9 persons. *Seasonable* from March to October.

## VEAL, Stewed with Peas, Young Carrots, and New Potatoes.

*Ingredients.*—3 or 4 lbs. of the loin or neck of veal, 15 young carrots, a few green onions, 1 pint of green peas, 12 new potatoes, a bunch of savoury herbs, pepper and salt to taste, 1 tablespoonful of lemon-juice, 2 tablespoonfuls of tomato sauce, 2 tablespoonfuls of mushroom ketchup. *Mode.*—Dredge the meat with flour, and roast or bake it for about ¾ hour: it should acquire a nice brown colour. Put the meat into a stewpan with the carrots, onions, potatoes, herbs, pepper, and salt; pour over it sufficient boiling water to cover it, and stew gently for 2 hours. Take out the meat and herbs, put it in a deep dish, skim off all the fat from the gravy, and flavour it with lemon-juice, tomato sauce, and mushroom ketchup, in the above proportion. Have ready a pint of green peas boiled *separately*; put these with the meat, pour over it the gravy, and serve. The dish may be garnished with a few forcemeat balls. The meat, when preferred, may be cut into chops, and floured and fried instead of being roasted; and any part of veal dressed in this way will be found extremely savoury and good. *Time.*—3 hours. *Average cost*, 9*d.* per lb. *Sufficient* for 6 or 7 persons. *Seasonable*, with peas, from June to August.

## VEGETABLE MARROW, Boiled.

**VEGETABLE MARROW ON TOAST.**

*Ingredients.*—To each ½ gallon of water, allow 1 heaped tablespoonful of salt; vegetable marrows. *Mode.*—Have ready a saucepan of boiling water, salted in the above proportion; put in the marrows after peeling them, and boil them until quite tender. Take them up with a slice, halve, and, should they be very large, quarter them. Dish them on toast, and send to table with them a tureen of molted butter, or, in lieu of this, a small pat of salt butter. Large vegetable marrows may be preserved throughout the winter by storing them in a dry place; when wanted for use, a few slices should be cut and boiled in the same manner as above; but, when once begun, the marrow must be eaten quickly, as it keeps but a short time after it is cut. Vegetable marrows are also very delicious mashed: they should be boiled, then drained, and mashed smoothly with a wooden spoon. Heat them in a saucepan, add a seasoning of salt and pepper, and a small piece of butter, and dish with a few sippets of toasted broad placed round as a garnish. *Time.*—Young vegetable marrows, 10 to 20 minutes; old ones, ½ to ¾ hour. *Average cost*, in full season, 1*s.* per dozen. *Sufficient.*—Allow 1 moderate-sized marrow for each person. *Seasonable* in July, August, and September; but may be preserved all the winter.

## VEGETABLE MARROW, Fried.

*Ingredients.*—3 medium-sized vegetable marrows, egg and bread-crumbs, hot lard. *Mode.*—Peel, and boil the marrows until tender in salt and water; then drain them and cut them in quarters, and take out the seeds. When thoroughly drained, brush the marrows over with egg, and sprinkle with bread-crumbs; have ready some hot lard, fry the marrow in this, and, when of a nice brown, dish; sprinkle over a little salt and pepper, and serve. *Time.*—About ½ hour to boil the marrow, 7 minutes to fry it. *Average cost*, in full season, 1s. per dozen. *Sufficient* for 4 persons. *Seasonable* in July, August, and September.

## VEGETABLE MARROWS IN WHITE SAUCE.

*Ingredients.*—4 or 5 moderate-sized marrows, ½ pint of white sauce. *Mode.*—Pare the marrows; cut them in halves, and shape each half at the top in a point, leaving the bottom end flat for it to stand upright in the dish. Boil the marrows in salt and water until tender; take them up very carefully, and arrange them on a hot dish. Have ready ½ pint of white sauce; pour this over the marrows, and serve. *Time.*—From 15 to 20 minutes to boil the marrows. *Average cost*, in full season, 1s. per dozen. *Sufficient* for 5 or 6 persons. *Seasonable* in July, August, and September.

**VEGETABLE MARROW IN WHITE SAUCE.**

## VEGETABLE MARROW SOUP.

*Ingredients.*—4 young vegetable marrows, or more, if very small, ½ pint of cream, salt and white pepper to taste, 2 quarts of white stock. *Mode.*—Pare and slice the marrows, and put them in the stock boiling. When done almost to a mash, press them through a sieve, and at the moment of serving, add the boiling cream and seasoning. *Time.*—1 hour. *Average cost,* 1s. 2d. per quart. *Seasonable* in summer. *Sufficient* for 8 persons.

## VEGETABLE SOUP.

*Ingredients.*—7 oz. of carrot, 10 oz. of parsnip, 10 oz. of potato, cut into thin slices; 1¼ oz. of butter, 5 teaspoonfuls of flour, a teaspoonful of made mustard, salt and pepper to taste, the yolks of 2 eggs, rather more than 2 quarts of water. *Mode.*—Boil the vegetables in the water 2½ hours; stir them often, and if the water boils away too quickly, add more, as there should be 2 quarts of soup when done. Mix up in a basin the butter and flour, mustard, salt, and pepper, with a teacupful of cold water; stir in the soup, and boil 10 minutes. Have ready the yolks of the eggs in the tureen; pour on, stir well, and serve. *Time.*—3 hours. *Average cost,* 4d. per quart. *Seasonable* in winter. *Sufficient* for 8 persons.

## VEGETABLE SOUP.

*Ingredients.*—Equal quantities of onions, carrots, turnips; ¼ lb. of butter, a crust of toasted bread, 1 head of celery, a faggot of herbs, salt and pepper to taste, 1 teaspoonful of powdered sugar, 2 quarts of common stock or boiling water. Allow ¾ lb. of vegetables to 2 quarts of stock. *Mode.*—Cut up the onions, carrots, and turnips; wash and drain them well, and put them in the stewpan with the butter and powdered sugar. Toss the whole over a sharp fire for 10 minutes, but do not let them brown, or you will spoil the flavour of the soup. When done, pour the stock or boiling water on them; add the bread, celery, herbs, and seasoning; stew for 3 hours; skim well and strain it off. When ready to serve, add a little sliced carrot, celery, and turnip, and flavour with a spoonful of Harvey's sauce, or a little ketchup. *Time.*—3½ hours. *Average cost,* 6d. per quart. *Seasonable* all the year. *Sufficient* for 8 persons.

## VEGETABLE SOUP. (*Good and Cheap, made without Meat.*)

*Ingredients.*—6 potatoes, 4 turnips, or 2 if very large; 2 carrots, 2 onions; if obtainable, 2 mushrooms; 1 head of celery, 1 large slice of bread, 1 small saltspoonful of salt, ¼ saltspoonful of ground black pepper, 2 teaspoonfuls of Harvey's sauce, 6 quarts of water. *Mode.*—Peel the vegetables, and cut them up into small pieces; toast the bread rather brown, and put all into a stewpan with the water and seasoning. Simmer gently for 3 hours, or until all is reduced to a pulp, and pass it through a sieve in the same way as pea-soup, which it should resemble in consistence; but it should be a dark brown colour. Warm it up again when required; put in the Harvey's sauce, and, if necessary, add to the flavouring. *Time.*—3 hours, or rather more. *Average cost*, 1*d.* per quart. *Seasonable* at any time. *Sufficient* for 16 persons.

*Note.*—This recipe was forwarded to the Editress by a lady in the county of Durham, by whom it was strongly recommended.

## VEGETABLES, Cut for Soups, &c.

The annexed engraving represents a cutter for shaping vegetables for soups, ragoûts, stews, &c.; carrots and turnips being the usual vegetables for which this utensil is used. Cut the vegetables into slices about ¼ inch in thickness, stamp them out with the cutter, and boil them for a few minutes in salt and water, until tender. Turnips should be cut in rather thicker slices than carrots, on account of the former boiling more quickly to a pulp than the latter.

**VEGETABLE-CUTTER.**

## VENISON, Hashed.

*Ingredients.*—The remains of roast venison, its own or mutton gravy, thickening of butter and flour. *Mode.*—Cut the meat from the bones in neat slices, and, if there is sufficient of its own gravy left, put the meat into this, as it is preferable to any other. Should there not be enough, put the bones and trimmings into a stewpan, with about a pint of mutton gravy; let them stew gently for an hour, and strain the gravy. Put a little flour and butter into the stewpan, keep stirring until brown, then add the strained gravy, and give it a boil up; skim and strain again, and, when a little cool, put in the slices of venison. Place the stewpan by the side of the fire, and, when on the point of simmering, serve: do not allow it to boil, or the meat will be hard. Send red-currant jelly to table with it. *Time.*—Altogether, 1½ hour. *Seasonable.* —Buck venison, from June to Michaelmas; doe venison, from November to the end of January.

*Note.*—A small quantity of Harvey's sauce, ketchup, or port wine, may be added to enrich the gravy: these ingredients must, however, be used very sparingly, or they will overpower the flavour of the venison.

## VENISON, Roast Haunch of.

**ROAST HAUNCH OF VENISON.**

*Ingredients.*—Venison, coarse flour-and-water paste, a little flour. *Mode.* —Choose a haunch with clear, bright, and thick fat, and the cleft of the hoof smooth and close; the greater quantity of fat there is, the better quality will the meat be. As many people object to venison when it has too much *haut goût*, ascertain how long it has been kept, by running a sharp skewer into the meat close to the bone: when this is withdrawn, its sweetness can be judged of. With care and attention, it will keep good a fortnight, unless the weather is very mild. Keep it perfectly dry by wiping it with clean cloths till not the least damp remains, and sprinkle over powdered ginger or pepper, as a preventive against the fly. When required for use, wash it in warm water, and *dry* it *well* with a cloth; butter a sheet of white paper, put it over the fat, lay a coarse paste, about ½ inch in thickness, over this, and then a sheet or two of strong paper. Tie the whole firmly on to the haunch with twine, and put the joint down to a strong close fire; baste the venison immediately, to prevent the paper and string from burning, and continue this operation, without intermission, the whole of the time it is cooking. About 20 minutes before it is done, carefully remove the paste and paper, dredge the joint with flour, and baste well with *butter* until it is nicely frothed, and of a nice pale-brown colour; garnish the knuckle-bone with a frill of white paper, and serve with a good, strong, but unflavoured gravy, in a tureen, and currant jelly; or melt the jelly with a little port, wine, and serve that also in a tureen. As the principal object in roasting venison is to preserve the fat, the above is the best mode of doing so where expense is not objected to; but, in ordinary cases, the paste may be dispensed with, and a double paper placed over the roast instead: it will not require so long cooking without the paste. Do not omit to send very hot plates to table, as the venison fat so soon freezes: to be thoroughly enjoyed by epicures, it should be eaten on hot-water plates. The neck and shoulder may be roasted in the same manner. *Time.*—A large haunch of buck venison, with the paste, 4 to 5 hours; haunch of doe venison, 3¼ to 3¾ hours. Allow less time without the paste. *Average cost*, 1*s*. 4*d*. to 1*s*. 6*d*. per lb. *Sufficient* for 18 persons. *Seasonable.* —Buck venison in greatest perfection from June to Michaelmas; doe venison from November to the end of January.

## VENISON, to Carve Haunch of.

Here is a grand dish for a knight of the carving-knife to exercise his skill upon, and, what will be pleasant for many to know, there is but little difficulty in the performance. An incision being made completely down to the bone, in the direction of the line 1 to 2, the gravy will then be able easily to flow; when slices, not too thick, should be cut along the haunch, as indicated by the line 4 to 3; that end of the joint marked 3 having been turned towards the carver, so that he may have a more complete command over the joint. Although some epicures affect to believe that some parts of the haunch are superior to others, yet we doubt if there is any difference between the slices cut above and below the line. It should be borne in mind to serve each guest with a portion of fat; and the most expeditious carver will be the best carver, as, like mutton, venison soon begins to chill, when it loses much of its charm.

**HAUNCH OF VENISON.**

## VENISON, Stewed.

*Ingredients.*—A shoulder of venison, a few slices of mutton fat, 2 glasses of port wine, pepper and allspice to taste, 1½ pint of weak stock or gravy, ½ teaspoonful of whole pepper, ½ teaspoonful of whole allspice. *Mode.*—Hang the venison till tender; take out the bone, flatten the meat with a rolling-pin, and place over it a few slices of mutton fat, which have been previously soaked for 2 or 3 hours in port wine; sprinkle these with a little fine allspice and pepper, roll the meat up, and bind and tie it securely. Put it into a stewpan with the bone and the above proportion of weak stock or gravy, whole allspice, black pepper, and port wine; cover the lid down closely, and simmer, very gently, from 3½ to 4 hours. When quite tender, take off the tape, and dish the meat; strain the gravy over it, and send it to table with red currant jelly. Unless the joint is very fat, the above is the best mode of cooking it. *Time.*—3½ to 4 hours. *Average cost*, 1*s*. 4*d*. to 1*s*. 6*d*. per lb. *Sufficient* for 10 or 12 persons. *Seasonable.*—Buck venison, from June to Michaelmas; doe venison, from November to the end of January.

## VERMICELLI PUDDING.

*Ingredients.*—4 oz. of vermicelli, 1½ pint of milk, ½ pint of cream, 3 oz. of butter, 3 oz. of sugar, 4 eggs. *Mode.*—Boil the vermicelli in the milk until it is tender; then stir in the remaining ingredients, omitting the cream, if not obtainable. Flavour the mixture with grated lemon-rind, essence of bitter almonds, or vanilla; butter a pie-dish; line the edges with puff-paste, put in the pudding, and bake in a moderate oven for about ¾ hour. *Time.*—¾ hour. *Average cost*, 1*s*. 2*d*. without cream. *Sufficient* for 5 or 6 persons. *Seasonable* at any time.

## VERMICELLI SOUP.

*Ingredients.*—1½ lb. of bacon, stuck with cloves; ½ oz. of butter, worked up in flour; 1 small fowl, trussed for boiling; 2 oz. of vermicelli, 2 quarts of white stock. *Mode.*—Put the stock, bacon, butter, and fowl, into the stewpan, and stew for ¾ of an hour. Take the vermicelli, add it to a little of the stock, and set it on the fire, till it is quite tender. When the soup is ready, take out the fowl and bacon, and put the bacon on a dish. Skim the soup as clean as possible; pour it, with the vermicelli, over the fowl. Cut some bread thin, put in the soup, and serve. *Time.*—2 hours. *Average cost*, exclusive of the fowl and bacon, 10*d.* per quart. *Seasonable* in winter. *Sufficient* for 4 persons.

## VERMICELLI SOUP.

*Ingredients.*—¼ lb. of vermicelli, 2 quarts of clear gravy stock. *Mode.*—Put the vermicelli in the soup, boiling; simmer very gently for ½ an hour, and stir frequently. *Time.*—½ an hour. *Average cost,* 1*s.* 3*d.* per quart. *Seasonable* all the year. *Sufficient* for 8 persons.

## VOL-AU-VENT (an Entrée).

*Ingredients.*—¾ to 1 lb. of puff-paste, fricasseed chickens, rabbits, ragoûts, or the remains of cold fish, flaked and warmed in thick white sauce. *Mode.*—Make from ¾ to 1 lb. of puff-paste, taking care that it is very evenly rolled out each time, to ensure its rising properly; and if the paste is not extremely light, and put into a good hot oven, this cannot be accomplished, and the *vol-au-vent* will look very badly. Roll out the paste to the thickness of about 1½ inch, and, with a fluted cutter, stamp it out to the desired shape, either round or oval, and, with the point of a small knife, make a slight incision in the paste all round the top, about an inch from the edge, which, when baked, forms the lid. Put the *vol-au-vent* into a good brisk oven, and keep the door shut for a few minutes after it is put in. Particular attention should be paid to the heating of the oven, for the paste *cannot* rise without a tolerable degree of heat. When of a nice colour, without being scorched, withdraw it from the oven, instantly remove the cover where it was marked, and detach all the soft crumb from the centre: in doing this, be careful not to break the edges of the *vol-au-vent*; but should they look thin in places, stop them with small flakes of the inside paste, stuck on with the white of an egg. This precaution is necessary to prevent the fricassee or ragoût from bursting the case, and so spoiling the appearance of the dish. Fill the *vol-au-vent* with a rich mince, or fricassee, or ragoût, or the remains of cold fish flaked and warmed in a good white sauce, and do not make them very liquid, for fear of the gravy bursting the crust: replace the lid, and serve. To improve the appearance of the crust, brush it over with the yolk of an egg *after* it has risen properly. *Time.*—¾ hour to bake the *vol-au-vent*. *Average cost*, exclusive of the interior, 1*s*. 6*d*. *Seasonable* at any time.

VOL-AU-VENT.

*Note.*—Small *vol-au-vents* may be made like those shown in the engraving, and filled with minced veal, chicken, &c. They should be made of the same paste as the larger ones, and stamped out with a small fluted cutter.

SMALL VOL-AU-VENTS.

## VOL-AU-VENT OF FRESH STRAWBERRIES, WITH WHIPPED CREAM.

*Ingredients.*—¾ lb. of puff-paste, 1 pint of freshly-gathered strawberries, sugar to taste, a plateful of whipped cream. *Mode.*—Make a *vol-au-vent* case, only not quite so large nor so high as for a savoury one. When nearly done, brush the paste over with the white of an egg, then sprinkle on it some pounded sugar, and put it back in the oven to set the glaze. Remove the interior, or soft crumb, and, at the moment of serving, fill it with the strawberries, which should be picked, and broken up with sufficient sugar to sweeten them nicely. Place a few spoonfuls of whipped cream on the top and serve. *Time.*—½ hour to 40 minutes to bake the *vol-au-vent*. *Average cost*, 2*s*. 3*d*. *Sufficient* for 1 *vol-au-vent*. *Seasonable* in June and July.

## VOL-AU-VENT, Sweet, of Plums, Apples, or any other Fresh Fruit.

*Ingredients.*—¾ lb. of puff-paste, about 1 pint of fruit compôte. *Mode.*—Make ½ lb. of puff-paste, taking care to bake it in a good brisk oven, to draw it up nicely and make it look light. Have ready sufficient stewed fruit, the syrup of which must be boiled down until very thick; fill the *vol-au-vent* with this, and pile it high in the centre; powder a little sugar over it, and put it back in the oven to glaze, or use a salamander for the purpose: the *vol-au-vent* is then ready to serve. It may be made with any fruit that is in season, such as rhubarb, oranges, gooseberries, currants, cherries, apples, &c.; but care must be taken not to have the syrup too thin, for fear of its breaking through the crust. *Time.*—½ hour to 40 minutes to bake the *vol-au-vent*. *Average cost*, exclusive of the compôte, 1s. 1d. *Sufficient* for 1 entremets.

## WAFERS, Geneva.

*Ingredients.*—2 eggs, 3 oz. butter, 3 oz. flour, 3 oz. pounded sugar. *Mode.*—Well whisk the eggs; put them into a basin, and stir to them the butter, which should be beaten to a cream; add the flour and sifted sugar gradually, and then mix all well together. Butter a baking-sheet, and drop on it a teaspoonful of the mixture at a time, leaving a space between each. Bake in a cool oven; watch the pieces of paste, and, when half done, roll them up like wafers, and put in a small wedge of bread or piece of wood, to keep them in shape. Return them to the oven until crisp. Before serving, remove the bread, put a spoonful of preserve in the widest end, and fill up with whipped cream. This is a very pretty and ornamental dish for the supper-table, and is very nice and easily made. *Time.*—Altogether from 20 to 25 minutes. *Average cost*, exclusive of the preserve and cream, 7d. *Sufficient* for a nice-sized dish. *Seasonable* at any time.

## WALNUT KETCHUP.

*Ingredients.*—100 walnuts, 1 handful of salt, 1 quart of vinegar, ¼ oz. of mace, ¼ oz. of nutmeg, ¼ oz. of cloves, ¼ oz. of ginger, ¼ oz. of whole black pepper, a small piece of horseradish, 20 shalots, ¼ lb. of anchovies, 1 pint of port wine. *Mode.*—Procure the walnuts at the time you can run a pin through them, slightly bruise, and put them into a jar with the salt and vinegar; let them stand 8 days, stirring every day; then drain the liquor from them, and boil it, with the above ingredients, for about ½ hour. It may be strained or not, as preferred, and, if required, a little more vinegar or wine can be added, according to taste. When bottled well, seal the corks. *Time.*—

½ hour. *Seasonable.*—Make this from the beginning to the middle of July, when walnuts are in perfection for pickling purposes.

## WALNUT KETCHUP.

*Ingredients.*—½ sieve of walnut-shells, 2 quarts of water, salt, ½ lb. of shalots, 1 oz. of cloves, 1 oz. of mace, 1 oz. of whole pepper, 1 oz. of garlic. *Mode.*—Put the walnut-shells into a pan, with the water, and a large quantity of salt; let them stand for 10 days, then break the shells up in the water, and let it drain through a sieve, putting a heavy weight on the top to express the juice; place it on the fire, and remove all scum that may arise. Now boil the liquor with the shalots, cloves, mace, pepper, and garlic, and let all simmer till the shalots sink; then put the liquor into a pan, and, when cold, bottle, and cork closely. It should stand 6 months before using: should it ferment during that time, it must be again boiled and skimmed. *Time.*—About ¾ hour. *Seasonable* in September, when the walnut-shells are obtainable.

## WALNUTS, to have Fresh throughout the Season.

*Ingredients.*—To every pint of water allow 1 teaspoonful of salt. *Mode.* —Place the walnuts in the salt and water for 24 hours at least; then take them out, and rub them dry. Old nuts may be freshened in this manner; or walnuts, when first picked, may be put into an earthen pan with salt sprinkled amongst them, and with damped hay placed on the top of them, and then covered down with a lid. They must be well wiped before they are put on table. *Seasonable.*—Should be stored away in September or October.

## WALNUTS, Pickled (very Good).

*Ingredients.*—100 walnuts, salt and water. To each quart of vinegar allow 2 oz. of whole black pepper, 1 oz. of allspice, 1 oz. of bruised ginger. *Mode.*—Procure the walnuts while young; be careful they are not woody, and prick them well with a fork; prepare a strong brine of salt and water (4 lbs. of salt to each gallon of water), into which put the walnuts, letting them remain 9 days, and changing the brine every third day; drain them off, put them on a dish, place it in the sun until they become perfectly black, which will be in 2 or 3 days; have ready dry jars, into which place the walnuts, and do not quite fill the jars. Boil sufficient vinegar to cover them, for 10 minutes, with spices in the above proportion, and pour it hot over the walnuts, which must be quite covered with the pickle; tie down with bladder, and keep in a dry place. They will be fit for use in a month, and will keep good 2 or 3 years. *Time.*—10 minutes. *Seasonable.*—Make this from the beginning to the middle of July, before the walnuts harden.

*Note.*—When liked, a few shalots may be added to the vinegar, and boiled with it.

## WATER SOUCHY.

Perch, tench, soles, eels, and flounders are considered the best fish for this dish. For the souchy, put some water into a stewpan with a bunch of chopped parsley, some roots, and sufficient salt to make it brackish. Let these simmer for 1 hour, and then stew the fish in this water. When they are done, take them out to drain, have ready some finely-chopped parsley, and a few roots cut into slices of about one inch thick and an inch in length. Put the fish in a tureen or deep dish, strain the liquor over them, and add the minced parsley and roots. Serve with brown bread and butter.

## WHEATEARS, to Dress.

*Ingredients.*—Wheatears; fresh butter. *Mode.*—After the birds are picked, gutted, and cleaned, truss them like larks, put them down to a quick fire, and baste them well with fresh butter. When done, which will be in about 20 minutes, dish them on fried bread-crumbs, and garnish the dish with slices of lemon. *Time.*—20 minutes. *Seasonable* from July to October.

## WHISKEY CORDIAL.

*Ingredients.*—1 lb. of ripe white currants, the rind of 2 lemons, ¼ oz. of grated ginger, 1 quart of whiskey, 1 lb. of lump sugar. *Mode.*—Strip the currants from the stalks; put them into a large jug; add the lemon-rind, ginger, and whiskey; cover the jug closely, and let it remain covered for 24 hours. Strain through a hair-sieve, add the lump sugar, and let it stand 12 hours longer; then bottle, and cork well. *Time.*—To stand 24 hours before being strained; 12 hours after the sugar is added. *Seasonable.*—Make this in July.

## WHITEBAIT, to Dress.

*Ingredients.*—A little flour, hot lard, seasoning of salt. *Mode.*—This fish should be put into iced water as soon as bought, unless they are cooked immediately. Drain them from the water in a colander, and have ready a nice clean dry cloth, over which put 2 good handfuls of flour. Toss in the whitebait, shake them lightly in the cloth, and put them in a wicker-sieve to take away the superfluous flour. Throw them into a pan of boiling lard, very few at a time, and let them fry till of a whitey-brown colour. Directly they are done, they must be taken out, and laid before the fire for a minute or two on a sieve reversed, covered with blotting-paper to absorb the fat. Dish them on a hot napkin, arrange the fish very high in the centre, and sprinkle a little salt over the whole. *Time.*—3 minutes. *Seasonable* from April to August.

## WHITE SAUCE, Good.

*Ingredients.*—½ pint of white stock, ½ pint of cream, 1 dessertspoonful of flour, salt to taste. *Mode.*—Have ready a delicately-clean saucepan, into which put the stock, which should be well flavoured with vegetables, and rather savoury; mix the flour smoothly with the cream, add it to the stock, season with a little salt, and boil all these ingredients very gently for about 10 minutes, keeping them well stirred the whole time, as this sauce is very liable to burn. *Time.*—10 minutes. *Average cost*, 1*s*. *Sufficient* for a pair of fowls. *Seasonable* at any time.

## WHITE SAUCE, Made without Meat.

*Ingredients.*—2 oz. of butter, 2 small onions, 1 carrot, ½ a small teacupful of flour, 1 pint of new milk, salt and cayenne to taste. *Mode.*—Cut up the onions and carrot very small, and put them into a stewpan with the butter; simmer them till the butter is nearly dried up; then stir in the flour, and add the milk; boil the whole gently until it thickens, strain it, season with salt and cayenne, and it will be ready to serve. *Time.*—¼ hour. *Average cost*, 5*d*. *Sufficient* for a pair of fowls. *Seasonable* at any time.

## WHITE SAUCE (a very Simple and Inexpensive Method).

*Ingredients.*—1½ pint of milk, 1½ oz. of rice, 1 strip of lemon-peel, 1 small blade of pounded mace, salt and cayenne to taste. *Mode.*—Boil the milk with the lemon-peel and rice until the latter is perfectly tender, then take out the lemon-peel and pound the milk and rice together; put it back into the stewpan to warm, add the mace and seasoning, give it one boil, and serve. This sauce should be of the consistency of thick cream. *Time.*—About 1½ hour to boil the rice. *Average cost*, 4d. *Sufficient* for a pair of fowls. *Seasonable* at any time.

## WHITING, Boiled.

*Ingredients.*—¼ lb. of salt to each gallon of water. *Mode.*—Cleanse the fish, but do not skin them; lay them in a fish-kettle, with sufficient cold water to cover them, and salt in the above proportion. Bring them gradually to a boil, and simmer gently for about 5 minutes, or rather more should the fish be very large. Dish them on a hot napkin, and garnish with tufts of parsley. Serve with anchovy or caper sauce, and plain melted butter. *Time.*—After the water boils, 5 minutes. *Average cost* for small whitings, 4d. each. *Seasonable* all the year, but best from October to March. *Sufficient.*—1 small whiting for each person.

To Choose Whiting.—Choose for the firmness of its flesh, and the silvery hue of its appearance.

## WHITING, Broiled.

*Ingredients.*—Salt and water; flour. *Mode.*—Wash the whiting in salt and water, wipe them thoroughly, and let them remain in the cloth to absorb all moisture. Flour them well, and broil over a very clear fire. Serve with *maître d'hôtel* sauce, or plain melted butter (*see* [Sauces](Sauces)). Be careful to preserve the liver, as by some it is considered very delicate. *Time.*—5 minutes for a small whiting. *Average cost*, 4d. each. *Seasonable* all the year, but best from October to March. *Sufficient.*—1 small whiting for each person.

## WHITING, &c.

Whiting, pike, haddock, and other fish, when of a sufficiently large size, may be carved in the same manner as salmon. When small, they may be cut through, bone and all, and helped in nice pieces, a middling-sized whiting serving for two slices.

## WHITING, Fried.

*Ingredients.*—Egg and bread-crumbs, a little flour, hot lard, or clarified dripping. *Mode.*—Take off the skin, clean, and thoroughly wipe the fish free from all moisture, as this is most essential, in order that the egg and bread-crumbs may properly adhere. Fasten the tail in the mouth by means of a small skewer, brush the fish over with egg, dredge with a little flour, and cover with bread-crumbs. Fry them in hot lard or clarified dripping of a nice colour, and serve them on a napkin, garnished with fried parsley. Send them to table with shrimp sauce and plain melted butter. *Time.*—-About 6 minutes. *Average cost*, 4d. each. *Seasonable* all the year, but best from October to March. *Sufficient.*—1 small whiting for each person.

*Note.*—Large whitings may be filleted, rolled, and served as fried filleted soles. Small fried whitings are frequently used for garnishing large boiled fish, such as turbot, cod, &c.

## WHITING AU GRATIN, or BAKED WHITING.

*Ingredients.*—4 whiting, butter, 1 tablespoonful of minced parsley, a few chopped mushrooms when obtainable; pepper, salt, and grated nutmeg to taste; butter, 2 glasses of sherry or Madeira, bread-crumbs. *Mode.*—Grease the bottom of a baking-dish with butter, and over it strew some minced parsley and mushrooms. Scale, empty, and wash the whitings, and wipe them thoroughly dry, carefully preserving the livers. Lay them in the dish, sprinkle them with bread-crumbs and seasoning, adding a little grated nutmeg, and also a little more minced parsley and mushrooms. Place small pieces of butter over the whiting, moisten with the wine, and bake for 20 minutes in a hot oven. If there should be too much sauce, reduce it by boiling over a sharp fire for a few minutes, and pour under the fish. Serve with a cut lemon, and no other sauce. *Time.*—20 minutes. *Average cost*, 4d. each. *Seasonable* all the year, but best from October to March. *Sufficient.*—This quantity for 4 or 5 persons.

## WHITING AUX FINES HERBES.

*Ingredients.*—1 bunch of sweet herbs chopped very fine; butter. *Mode.*—Clean and skin the fish, fasten the tails in the mouths, and lay them in a baking-dish. Mince the herbs very fine, strew them over the fish, and place small pieces of butter over; cover with another dish, and let them simmer in a Dutch oven for ¼ hour or 20 minutes. Turn the fish once or twice, and serve with the sauce poured over. *Time.*—¼ hour or 20 minutes. *Average cost*, 4d. each. *Seasonable* all the year, but best from October to March. *Sufficient.*—1 small whiting for each person.

## WIDGEON, Roast.

*Ingredients.*—Widgeons, a little flour, butter. *Mode.*—These are trussed in the same manner as wild duck, but must not be kept so long before they are dressed. Put them down to a brisk fire; flour, and baste them continually with butter, and, when browned and nicely frothed, send them to table hot and quickly. Serve with brown gravy, or orange gravy, and a cut lemon. *Time.*—¼ hour; if liked well done, 20 minutes. *Average cost*, 1s. each: but seldom bought. *Sufficient.*—2 for a dish. *Seasonable* from October to February.

## WIDGEON.

Widgeon may be carved in the same way as described in regard to wild duck.

## WINE OR BRANDY SAUCE FOR PUDDINGS.

*Ingredients.*—1 pint of melted butter, 3 heaped teaspoonfuls of pounded sugar; 1 *large* wineglassful of port or sherry, or ¾ of a *small* glassful of brandy. *Mode.*—Make ½ pint of melted butter, omitting the salt; then stir in the sugar and wine or spirit in the above proportion, and bring the sauce to the point of boiling. Serve in a boat or tureen separately, and, if liked, pour a little of it over the pudding. To convert this into punch sauce, add to the sherry and brandy a small wineglassful of rum and the juice and grated rind of ½ lemon. Liqueurs, such as Maraschino or Curaçoa, substituted for the brandy, make excellent sauces. *Time.*—Altogether, 15 minutes. *Average cost*, 8*d*. *Sufficient* for 6 or 7 persons.

## WINE SAUCE FOR PUDDINGS.

*Ingredients.*—½ pint of sherry, ¼ pint of water, the yolks of 5 eggs, 2 oz. of pounded sugar, ½ teaspoonful of minced lemon-peel, a few pieces of candied citron cut thin. *Mode.*—Separate the yolks from the whites of 5 eggs; beat them, and put them into a very clean saucepan (if at hand, a lined one is best); add all the other ingredients, place them over a sharp fire, and keep stirring until the sauce begins to thicken; then take it off and serve. If it is allowed to boil, it will be spoiled, as it will immediately curdle. *Time.*—To be stirred over the fire 3 or 4 minutes; but it must not boil. *Average cost*, 2*s*. *Sufficient* for a large pudding; allow half this quantity for a moderate-sized one. *Seasonable* at any time.

## WINE SAUCE FOR PUDDINGS, Excellent.

*Ingredients.*—The yolks of 4 eggs, 1 teaspoonful of flour, 2 oz. of pounded sugar, 2 oz. of fresh butter, ¼ saltspoonful of salt, ½ pint of sherry or Madeira. *Mode.*—Put the butter and flour into a saucepan, and stir them over the fire until the former thickens; then add the sugar, salt, and wine, and mix these ingredients well together. Separate the yolks from the whites of 4 eggs; beat up the former, and stir them briskly to the sauce; let it remain over the fire until it is on the point of simmering; but do not allow it to boil, or it will instantly curdle. This sauce is delicious with plum, marrow, or bread puddings; but should be served separately, and not poured over the pudding. *Time.*—From 5 to 7 minutes to thicken the butter; about 5 minutes to stir the sauce over the fire. *Average cost*, 1*s*. 10*d*. *Sufficient* for 7 or 8 persons.

## WINE, to Mull.

*Ingredients.*—To every pint of wine allow 1 large cupful of water, sugar, and spice to taste. *Mode.*—In making preparations like the above, it is very difficult to give the exact proportions of ingredients like sugar and spice, as what quantity might suit one person would be to another quite distasteful. Boil the spice in the water until the flavour is extracted, then add the wine and sugar, and bring the whole to the boiling-point, when serve with strips of crisp dry toast, or with biscuits. The spices usually used for mulled wine are cloves, grated nutmeg, and cinnamon or mace. Any kind of wine may be mulled, but port and claret are those usually selected for the purpose; and the latter requires a very large proportion of sugar. The vessel that the wine is boiled in must be delicately clean, and should be kept exclusively for the purpose. Small tin warmers may be purchased for a trifle, which are more suitable than saucepans, as, if the latter are not scrupulously clean, they will spoil the wine, by imparting to it a very disagreeable flavour. These warmers should be used for no other purposes.

## WOODCOCK, Roast.

*Ingredients.*—Woodcocks; butter, flour, toast. *Mode.*—Woodcocks should not be drawn, as the trails are, by epicures, considered a great delicacy. Pluck, and wipe them well outside; truss them with the legs close to the body, and the feet pressing upon the thighs; skin the neck and head, and bring the beak round under the wing. Place some slices of toast in the dripping-pan to catch the trails, allowing a piece of toast for each bird. Roast before a clear fire from 15 to 25 minutes; keep them well basted, and flour and froth them nicely. When done, dish the pieces of toast with the birds upon them, and pour round a very little gravy; send some more to table in a tureen. These are most delicious birds when well cooked; but they should not be kept too long: when the feathers drop, or easily come out, they are fit for for table. *Time.*—When liked underdone, 15 to 20 minutes; if liked well done, allow an extra 5 minutes. *Average cost.*—Seldom bought. *Sufficient.*—2 for a dish. *Seasonable* from November to February.

ROAST WOODCOCK.

## WOODCOCK.

This bird, like a partridge, may be carved by cutting it exactly into two like portions, or made into three helpings, as described in carving partridge. The backbone is considered the tit-bit of a woodcock, and by many the thigh is also thought a great delicacy. This bird is served in the manner advised by Brillat Savarin, in connection with the pheasant, viz., on toast which has received its drippings whilst roasting; and a piece of this toast should invariably accompany each plate.

WOODCOCK.

## WOODCOCK, SCOTCH.

*Ingredients.*—A few slices of hot buttered toast; allow 1 anchovy to each slice. For the sauce,—¼ pint of cream, the yolks of 3 eggs. *Mode.*—Separate the yolks from the whites of the eggs; beat the former, stir to them the cream, and bring the sauce to the boiling-point, but do not allow it to boil, or it will curdle. Have ready some hot buttered toast, spread with anchovies pounded to a paste; pour a little of the hot sauce on the top, and serve very hot and very quickly. *Time.*—5 minutes to make the sauce hot. *Sufficient.*—Allow ½ slice to each person. *Seasonable* at any time.

## YEAST-CAKE.

*Ingredients.*—1½ lb. of flour, ½ lb. of butter, ½ pint of milk, 1½ tablespoonful of good yeast, 3 eggs, ¾ lb. of currants, ½ lb. of white moist sugar, 2 oz. of candied peel. *Mode.*—Put the milk and butter into a saucepan, and shake it round over a fire until the butter is melted, but do not allow the milk to get very hot. Put the flour into a basin, stir to it the milk and butter, the yeast and eggs, which should be well beaten, and form the whole into a smooth dough. Let it stand in a warm place, covered with a cloth, to rise, and, when sufficiently risen, add the currants, sugar, and candied peel cut into thin slices. When all the ingredients are thoroughly mixed, line 2 moderate-sized cake-tins with buttered paper, which should be about six inches higher than the tin; pour in the mixture, let it stand to rise again for another ½ hour, and then bake the cakes in a brisk oven for about 1½ hour. If the tops of them become too brown, cover them with paper until they are done through. A few drops of essence of lemon, or a little grated nutmeg, may be added when the flavour is liked. *Time.*—From 1¼ to 1½ hour. *Average cost*, 2s. *Sufficient* to make 2 moderate-sized cakes. *Seasonable* at any time.

## YEAST-DUMPLINGS.

*Ingredients.*—½ quartern of dough, boiling water. *Mode.*—Make a very light dough as for bread, using to mix it, milk, instead of water; divide it into 7 or 8 dumplings; plunge them into boiling water, and boil them for 20 minutes. Serve the instant they are taken up, as they spoil directly, by falling and becoming heavy; and in eating them do not touch them with a knife, but tear them apart with two forks. They may be eaten with meat gravy, or cold butter and sugar; and if not convenient to make the dough at home, a little from the baker's answers as well, only it must be placed for a few minutes near the fire, in a basin with a cloth over it, to let it rise again before it is made into dumplings. *Time.*—20 minutes. *Average cost*, 4d. *Sufficient* for 5 or 6 persons. *Seasonable* at any time.

## YEAST, to Make, for Bread.

*Ingredients.*—1½ oz. of hops, 3 quarts of water, 1 lb. of bruised malt, ½ pint of yeast. *Mode.*—Boil the hops in the water for 20 minutes; let it stand for about 5 minutes, then add it to 1 lb. of bruised malt prepared as for brewing. Let the mixture stand covered till about lukewarm; then put in not quite ½ pint of yeast; keep it warm, and let it work 3 or 4 hours; then put it into small ½-pint bottles (ginger-beer bottles are the best for the purpose), cork them well, and tie them down. The yeast is now ready for use; it will keep good for a few weeks, and 1 bottle will be found sufficient for 18 lbs. of flour. When required for use, boil 3 lbs. of potatoes without salt, mash them in the same water in which they were boiled, and rub them through a colander. Stir in about ½ lb. of flour; then put in the yeast, pour it in the middle of the flour, and let it stand warm on the hearth all night, and in the morning let it be quite warm when it is kneaded. The bottles of yeast require very careful opening, as it is generally exceedingly ripe. *Time.*—20 minutes to boil the hops and water, the yeast to work 3 or 4 hours. *Sufficient.*—½ pint sufficient for 18 lbs. of flour.

## YEAST, Kirkleatham.

*Ingredients.*—2 oz. of hops, 4 quarts of water, ½ lb. of flour, ½ pint of yeast. *Mode.*—Boil the hops and water for 20 minutes; strain, and mix with the liquid ½ lb. of flour and not quite ½ pint of yeast. Bottle it up, and tie the corks down. When wanted for use, boil potatoes according to the quantity of bread to be made (about 3 lbs. are sufficient for about a peck of flour); mash them, add to them ½ lb. of flour, and mix about ½ pint of the yeast with them; let this mixture stand all day, and lay the bread to rise the night before it is wanted. *Time.*—20 minutes to boil the hops and water. *Sufficient.*—½ pint of this yeast sufficient for a peck of flour, or rather more.